EXCAVATION AT KARKABHAT - CHHATTISGARH

(A Megalithic Site)

EXCAVATION AT KARKABHAT - CHHATTISGARH

(A Megalithic Site)

A.K. SHARMA

AGAM

AGAM KALA PRAKASHAN

DELHI

First Published : 2010

ISBN :978- 81-7320-103-5

Published by :
Dr. Agam Prasad, M.A., Ph.D., Diploma in Museology
for Agam Kala Prakashan
34, Central Market, Ashok Vihar, Delhi-110052
Ph. : 27212195, 47098550, 65688806-7
Fax : 91-11-27212195
E-mail : agambooks@gmail.com, agambook@yahoo.com
Website : www.agamkala.com

Laser Typesetting by :
Elegant Printographics
319, IIIrd Floor, R.G. Complex-I,
Sector-14, Rohini, Delhi-85.
Ph. : 9891247305

Printed at :
Chawla Offset
Wazirpur Village, Ashok Vihar,
Delhi-110052

Printed in India

Dedicated to the
sweet memories of
My Mother
and other family members
and to the students of
Institute of Archaeology

— *A.K. Sharma*

PREFACE

Right from my childhood, when people use to call Chhattisgarh as one of the most backward area of India, my concense did not allow me to believe this. I wondered how this god gifted land with very fertile soil, abundance of forest and mineral wealth, highly disciplined and skilled people could be called backward. Just because no body even attempted to unearth the hidden past, the area can not be branded as backward.

In 1990 when I got chance to work independently in Pre-history Branch of Archaeological Survey of India, my first target was to excavate a sprawling megalithic site in Chhattisgarh and I chose Karkabhat. The attempt was amply rewarded. Now with more excavations the glorious past of this region has started coming out.

For giving me opportunity I am grateful to the Director General, Archaeological Survey of India. For giving me moral support, I am indebted to the people of Karkabhat and around and to the media, particularly to "Surabhi" team for immediately telecasting the startling results on 'Doordarshan' to the viewers.

I have sweet memories of my mother and my other family members, who though for a short time, lived with me in the excavation camp at Karkabhat and encouraged me. In fact, I could carry out this excavation as cool comfort of my mother's lap was available to me.

Regarding our camp, seeing the sprawling tents and presence of staff and students of both the batches of Institute of Archaeology, Archaeological Survey of India, Shri Chandulal Chandrakar, Chief Correspondent. "Hindustan Times" remarked, "it looks like the camp of Tipu Sultan."

I did my best to give as much as possible exposure to the students in a so-called backward region. They still remember this rewarding forty days in Chhattisgarh, because I believe field exposure is the only way to learn archaeology.

I am sure students and scholars will benefit from our efforts. Gone are the days when there used to be proper training in large scale excavations. Let us hop the interest will revive.

Raipur **A.K. Sharma**

Akshaya Tritiya, 2067

16th May, 2010

ACKNOWLEDGEMENTS

The excavations at Karkabhat was carried out by the Prehistory Branch of Archaeological Survey of India, under my direction and with assistance from S/Shri S.B.Ota, S.K. Lekhwani, S.S. Gupta, N.G. Nikosey and R.S. Rana. The report on iron objects has been contributed by Shri S.S. Gupta. The drawings were prepared by S/Shri J.S. Dubey, K.M. Girhe, R.K. Dwivedi and Lal Singh. Photographs were taken by S/Shri R.S. Rana, Pyara Singh and N.K.Nimje. To them I am deeply beholden for their ungrudging assistance. I am also grateful to S/Shri C.L. Yadav, S.M. Shambharkar, P.S. Pashine, V.W. Pathak, P.C. Dogra, Smt. K.V. Rao, R.G. Katole, T.B. Thapa and R.S. Sharma for their untiring work. For the final typescript my thanks are due to Shri P.V. Janardhanan.

I am grateful to Shri M.C. Joshi, Director General, Archaeological Survey of India for giving opportunigy, required guidance and facilities to take up this excavation.

LIST OF ILLUSTRATIONS

Figures

Plates

CONTENTS

1

THE BACKGROUND

Megalithic culture in India dates back from the later half of second millenium B.C. to 1st/2nd century B.C. Remains of this culture are available right from Kashmir valley to down south in Kerala and from Manipur to Rajasthan. At Buzahoun,[1] Gufkral[2] and many other sites, free standing memorial stones, called menhirs, have been discovered. At Leh[3] in Laddakh, graves made of stone slabs are reported. At Asota near Murdan in N.W. Frontier Province of Pakistan there is a group of menhirs arranged in some rough alignment. In fact it now appears that it was from second half of second millenium B.C. to nearly second half of first millenium B.C. that the Indian sub-continent was for the first time more culturally united. As per evidence, megalithic people are known for growing rice and smelting of iron for the first time in our sub-continent. The most important feature of this culture is erection of huge burials and/or memorial stones for their departed souls. Many types of such burials are known from different parts of India.

The tradition of erecting memorial columns still continues amongst various tribes in north-east India and Central India. Memorial stones varying in sizes and shapes were put up in honour of the departed souls. The Nagas still put up in honour of some great man or event or to commemorate some meritorious act. Marias and Murias of Bastar (Chhattisgarh), various Naga tribes and others erect such columns, in the form of 'buffalo horns', 2 to 2.5m high wooden 'shields' cut in the form of 'U' and covered with beautiful intricate carvings comprising of men, animals, sun and moon, etc. Rengma Nagas use rows of stones, gradually decreasing in size. In Garo Hills such wooden pillars are set up before houses in memory of the departed souls.

In August, 1991, an elaborate ceremony lasting for several days was organised by a section of tribes in Bastar. In this ceremony thousands of people from the neighbouring region of Andhra Pradesh and Maharashtra also participated. The ceremony was organised after a gap of nearly twentyfive years wherein stone menhirs were erected by the relatives of the deceased (in about last twentyfive years) at a particular selected spot. Each family willing to erect a memorial was required to contribute one quintal of rice for the mass feasting. Rice was cooked in furrows dug in the earth and no earthern or metal pot was involved in the cooking process. It was as simple like this. On a plain ground nearly half a meter deep and two meter long furrows were dug up. The floor of these furrows were lined with dry twigs which in turn were covered with broad thick green leaves, preferably of teak or Pallas, over which nearly 10 cm thick layer of water soaked raw rice was speard. The layer of rice was again covered with green leaves and then dry twigs. The entire furrow was then covered with a thin layer of earth. Before putting layer of earth the twigs were fired. In about half an hour time, by the process of slow cooking under controlled atmosphere, steaming hot well cooked rice was available to serve.

Similar such customs could be traced throughout upto Nagaland and Manipur.

Struck with the similarity of customs of erecting menhirs right from 1500 B.C. till this date in various geographical zones of the country, explorations were recently undertaken to locate such sites in Chhattisgarh and South Bihar in order to fill up the gap in these regions. Latest discoveries of extensive megalithic sites in Durg district at Tengana (20°34'45" N Lat., 81°21'20% E Long.) and in Dhamtari district at Aroud-Lilar-Bhawarmara (20°41'N Lat., 81°39' E Long.) on the right bank of Mahanadi east of Dhamtari; at Bartia Bhata (21°22'30" N Lat., 82°55'20" E Long.) near Basna in Mahasamund district and in Hazaribagh district of Bihar in Damodar valley at Phatha (24°55' N Lat., 85°19'E

Long.), Pakri-Barwadih (23°52' N Lat., 85°13' E Long.); Bhagwantar (23°44' N Lat., 85°3' E Long.), Senti/ Kaharzardi Tola (23°48' N Lat., 85°2' E Long.); Mandar (23°47' N Lat., 85°2' E Long.), indicate that the gap is only due to lack of investigations. Sprawling sites of Karkabhat region and Aroud region are amongst the biggest sites in India, both area wise and typologically.

First ever mention about the megaliths around Karkabhat has been made by J.D. Beglar[4] in his report on a tour in the Central Provinces, which he undertook in 1873-74. He mentions "From the village of Navapara to Majhgaon runs a long stretch of broken blocks of stones lying loose on each other in irregular masses, and presenting the exact appearance of the ruins of a great fort two miles long; at intervals stand upright stones looking like sati pillars; the whole present an appearance of desolation unrivalled even by the ruins of Delhi. I could, however, find no ground on examination to consider this the site of a fort or of a great town; it appears to be the remains of a quarry. The general surface of the country for sone miles is gravelly, with extensive plains of laterite, while here crops up granite, and it is possible therefore that stone for building the temples in and for a considerable distance around the place as Balod, Sorar, Gowror, etc. was obtained hence". Beglar never imagined them to be menhirs or megaliths as at that time the knowledge about this culture has not developed.

The first recognition of these sites came in 1933-34,[5] wherein they were described as Stone Age Cemetery (?) and were declared as Protected Monuments. The report mentions, "Near Sorar, Chirchari, Karkabhat, Majagahan and Karhibhadar, all in the Durg district, there are large areas of what can tentatively be called a stone Age Cemetery, though neither the age nor the purpose of these remnants are known. These areas are covered with a large quantity of stones, evidently heaped up by man, and here and there a huge megalith standing erect as if to mark a grave (?) - - No excavations have so far been carried out under the boulders. All the five villages are situated within a circuit of about 5 to 6 miles. Local people know no stories or legends connected with these mouments. There is no writing, carving or engraving on any of the upright stones. They have been declared Protected Monuments and further investigation is indicated".

Years passed and no attempts were made to excavate one or two of them to know their antiquity. Even after independence the area remained totally neglected as first it was under the jurisdiction of Patna Circle then was transferred to South-Eastern Circle, Hyderabad, and then to Central Circle, Bhopal and ultimately to Bhubaneswar Circle. As the headquarters were far away, the area remained totally neglacted.

It was in 1956-57, that under Dr. M.G. Dikshit of the Madhya Pradesh Department of Archaeology excavatios were carried out in the megalithic area at Dhanora[6]

Dhanora is located 21 kms. from Balod on Balod-Dhamtari road. During the time of excavation nearly 500 megaliths were located. The purpose of excavation as mentioned by Dr. Dikshit was 'with a view to ascertain their nature and possible connections with the megaliths of peninsular India and links, if any, with their counterparts prevaling among the present-day aboriginals of Bastar'. He classified the megaliths under four types : Type, I : apsidal stone enclosure with a capstone lying flush on a heap of cairn; Type II: apsidal stone enclosure around a menhir at its centre, ranging from 5 to 7 feet in height, and a smaller one, 3 to 4 feet in height, situated at a distance of 6 to 7 feet to the south of the former, Type III: alignment of apsidal stone enclosures like type II, occuring in groups of five to seven; and Type IV, menhirs, often of huge proportions, kept in position by means of butteresses of large boulders.

Four megliths, three of Type I and one of Type II were excavated. The excavation of the Type I revealed that the apsidal enclosures surrounded a burial pit on all sides except the southern side which was kept open; covered by a cairn packing with a capstone lying flush on a cairn heap. The pit generally contained a few fragments of skeletal remains, besides objects like beads and glass bangles, but no pottery. One of the tombs contained a copper vessel. The capstone measured 10 to 15 feet in length, 4 to 5 feet in width and 2 to 3 feet in thickness.

The excavation of an apsidal enclosure of Type II showed that the menhirs, oriented north-south, were supported by a packing of rubble and clay. As no object was associated with them, they probably served only as memorial-stones.

Though the groups of megaliths were discovered in 1873-74, described in detail in 1933-34 (with photographs), and then excavated in 1956-57, it is a pity that they were again reported to have been located in 1972-73 by Prof. K.D. Bajpai, Dr. S.K. Pandey and Shri S.N. Manwami of the Department of Ancient Indian History, Culture and archaeology, University of Sagar.[7]

The present region of Chhattisgarh comprising Raipur, Bilaspur, Raigarh, Sarguja, Bastar, Durg, Rajnandgaon and recently created districts of Chattisgarh was known as Dakshina Kosala in ancient historical times. Prior to that evidences of occupation by early man right from Early Stone Age to megalithic times through Middle Stone Age, Late stone age and Neolithic times are available in this region.

After indepencdence, this region also could not remain untouched by developmental activities, though meager. Dams and roads came up. For the construction of these, millions of stone ballast was required and it is these groups of menhirs and cairn heaps which fell prey to the greedy contractors. It was easy and more profitable to convert these megalithic monuments into ballast than to quarry fresh stones from exposed and unexposed rocks. When the area was visited in July, 1990, out of 500 megaliths, reported by Dr. M.G. Dikshit in 1956-57, not a single was standing or presnt. Those at Chirchuri, Mujgahan, Sorar and Karhibhadar were totally wiped out except few at Mujgahan.

Forest department was equally responsible for their destruction as these stones were freely usd to demarcate the boundaries of forest zones. Use by these agencies in still going unchecked as the government has turned a blind eye due to money and political power. If timely action is not taken megaliths will be wiped out from Chhattisgarh.

Fortunately, a major portion at Karkabhat had escaped destruction, except nearly one fourth which were destroyed by the construction of Balod-Dhamtari road which passes right over them.

I was fortunate enough to discover a sprawling megalithic site just 4 kms. south of Dhanora at Tengna[8] on 3.6.1990. This site escaped the notice of earlier explorers as those days the area was covered with thick forest infested with wild animals and had no approach road. But now this site is also on the verge of extinction due to ballast making.

Dr. Dikshit's excavation at Dhanora was only limited. In the absence of any large scale excavations of any megalithic site in Chhattisgarh region their antiquity was neither properly understood nor their links with megalithic remains and culture of other regions established. In order to make an attempt to find out answers to these questions, it was decided to undertake excavations at Karkabhat. Another reason was the fast disappearing sites in the area due to deforestation, urbanization and other developmental activities in the area.

References

1. *Indian Archaeology* 1960-61, *A Review*, p. 11.
2. *Indian Archaeology* 1981-2, A Review, p.
3. Franchke, A.H., *Annual Report of Archaeological Survey of India*, 1909-10, p. 104.
4. Beglar J.D., *Report on a tour in Bundelkhand and Malwa,* 1871-72, *and in the central Provinces* 1873-74, Archaeological Survey of India, Vol.VII, Calcutta, 1878,, p. 188.
5. *Annual Reports of the Archaeological Survey of India, for the years* 1930-31, 1931-32, 1932-33 and 1933-34, Part I, pp. 141-42, Part II, Plates LXXVII, b, c & d, Delhi, 1936. Ed. Fabri C.L.
6. Dikshit M.G., *Excavations at Dhanora,* District Durg, in *Indian Archaeology* 1956-57-A Review, p. 35.
7. *Indian Archaeology* 1972-73-*A review, Exploration in District Durg*, pp. 14-15, New Delhi, 1978.
8. *Indian Archaeology* 1990-91-*A review*, Exploration *in District durg* - Unpublished.

2

GEOLOGY AND ENVIRONMENT

The geological formation in the area dates back from Archaean times to recent Pleistocine.[1] So far as the megalithic culture is concerned, we have to deal partly with the upper cretacious formation of Deccan trap and recent Pleistocine formations of lateritic bed, older alluvium and alluvial soils. There are extensive horizontal types of gritty and conglomaratic quartzite and fine purplish sand stone with spots of green chlorite and pink to buff shales. The Deccan trap consists of several flows of baslats. The laterite is mainly found capping the Deccan trap. It occurs at plaçes over the ferrugenuous shales and epidiorites. Boulders and pebbles of laterite occur in high hills. In southern and south-western part of the Durg district are the lower extension of Bastar plateau interpursed by a few hills. It lies in an elevation of 381 metres. The hills of this region extend from the south, on the region between rivers and gradually merge with the plain in the north. The central region between Kharkara and the Tandula is important for presence of Rajhara hills of iron ore at the heigh of 584.9mtr. East of theTandula, the highest peak is 597.4 metres near Markatola. The main river of this district Shivnath forms part of the Shivnath-Mahanadi drainage system. The drainage in the whole of the district is the result of long erosion of old hard masses.

A. Minerals[2]

Copper Ore

Encrustations of copper-carbonates have been found in the galina-quartz vein transversing the gniessis near Chicholi. Similar traces were found in a quartz vein at Wara-Band (21°04'., 80°50').

Iron Ore

Iron ore deposits are confined to Dalli-Rajhara range of hills in the south-western part of the district. There are reserves in Dondi-Lohara area also. The percentage of iron varies from 69 to 66.35%. South and south-west of Jharandalli the banded hematite-quartzites of Iron-ore series are exposed. Dalli is most advantageously situated as regards the supply of water. There are several springs in the neighbourhood yielding it in a very pure form. The ores have been worked in open furnaces by indegeneous methods, being mixed with charcoal in the preparation one part of ore into 3 of charcoal. In the Sanjari-Balod tahsil 19 of such furnaces have worked in 1907. The metal turned out by the furnaces was refined in an open hearth and is made into bars called *Chuls* which were sold to blacksmiths. The workers were Agarias, a branch of Gonds. The occurance of laterites used for indigenous iron-smelting may be mentioned at Nandinitola, Akalberia and Rajdhar villages of Durg District.[1]

Lead and Silver

Galena has been known to occur in veins and stringers of quartz at Thelkadand (20°37'., 89°45'). Quartz veins with galena, have also been noticed in the laminated shales at Karantara (20°41'., 80°48') in Ambagarh chowki area. Lead has also been reported from the Chandi Dongri shear zone where a quartz vein has been traced for over a kilometre. Specimen of ore yielded over 9 oz. of silver pattern leads. An outcrop of quartz veins with lead and copper ores occurs in a country of shale and green stone west of Murhipar (21°21'., 80°52').

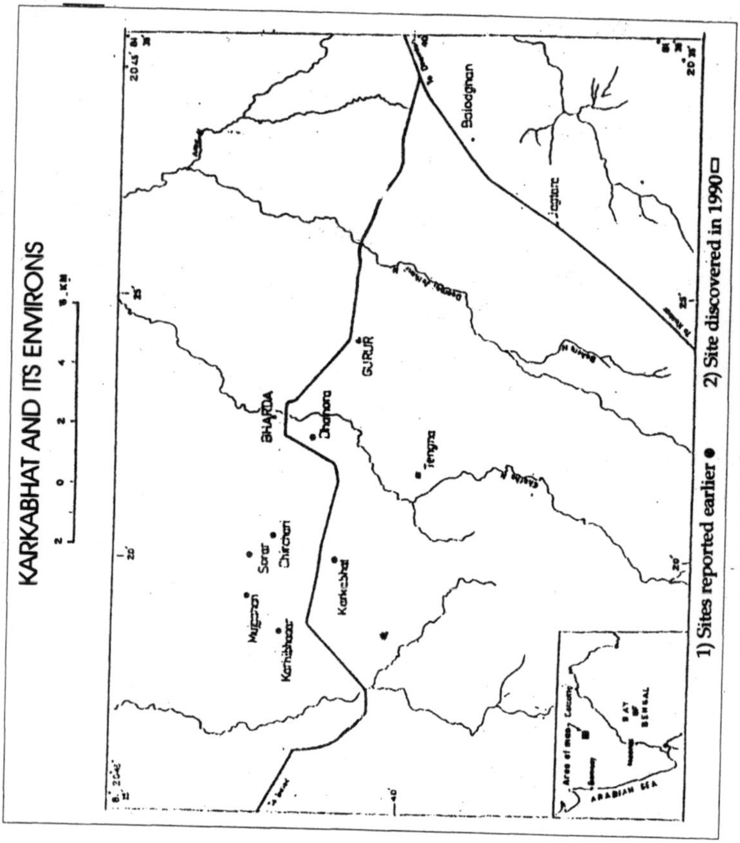

Fig. 1 : Karkabhat and its environs

Gold

It is found in the Khairgarh tahsil of Rajnandgaon district as well as in the Jonk river in Raipur district.

Ochre

Red ochre of finest quality is obtained from pits of Gandai and Thakurtola area. Yellow and brown ochreous enrichments have frequently been noticed in the ferrugeneous shelves of the Sanjari-Balod tahsil.

B. Fauna

Monkey (Semnopithecus entellus-*Kalmuha Bendra*); Tiger (Felis panthera-*sher, bagh*); Panther (Panthera pardus - *tendua, chitwa*); Leopard (Acinonyx Jubata-*chita*); Indian civet (Viverra Malaccensis-bignaore); mangoose (Herpestes edwardsi, Geoffrey-*newara*); Indian otter (Lutra lutra vulgaris); the striped hyaena (Hyaena striata-*rerwa*); Indian wolves (Canis lupus-*hundra*); Jackal (Cahis aureus-*kolhia*); Indian wild dog (Cyon dukhunen sis-*khekri*); Indian fox (Vulpes bengalensis-*khekri*); Indian sloth-bear (Melursus ursinus-*bhaluwa*); Indian hare (Lepus ruficaudatus-*lamha*); Indian boar (Sus cristatus-*barha*); The nilgai (Boselephus tragocamelus-*rojra*); the four-horned antelope (Tetracerus quadricornis-charsinga); barking deer (Cervulus muntjac-bhasera); spotted deer (Axis axis) and the Sambhar (Cervus unicolor) are the common animals found in the forests of this area.

Amongst the birds the common peafowl (Pavo cristatus), the common jungle cock (Gallus gallus), the common spur-fowls (Galloperdix spadicea); the painted spur-fowls (Galloperdix lunulata), the painted francolin (Francolinus francolinus); the rock or painted sand-groues (Pteoloculurus exustus), the jungle or bush-quail (Pedicula Asiatica) are found in the plains, jungles and rocks of the area.

References

1. India-A Regional Geography, Chhattisgarh Region, p. 735; Ed. Singh R.L., Varanasi, 1971.
2. Gazetteer of India, M.P., Durg District, Ed. Dr. Verma Rajendra, Bhopal, 1972, pp. 16-19.
3. India, A Regional Geography, Chhattisgarh region, p. 741. Ed.Singh R.L., Varanasi, 1971.

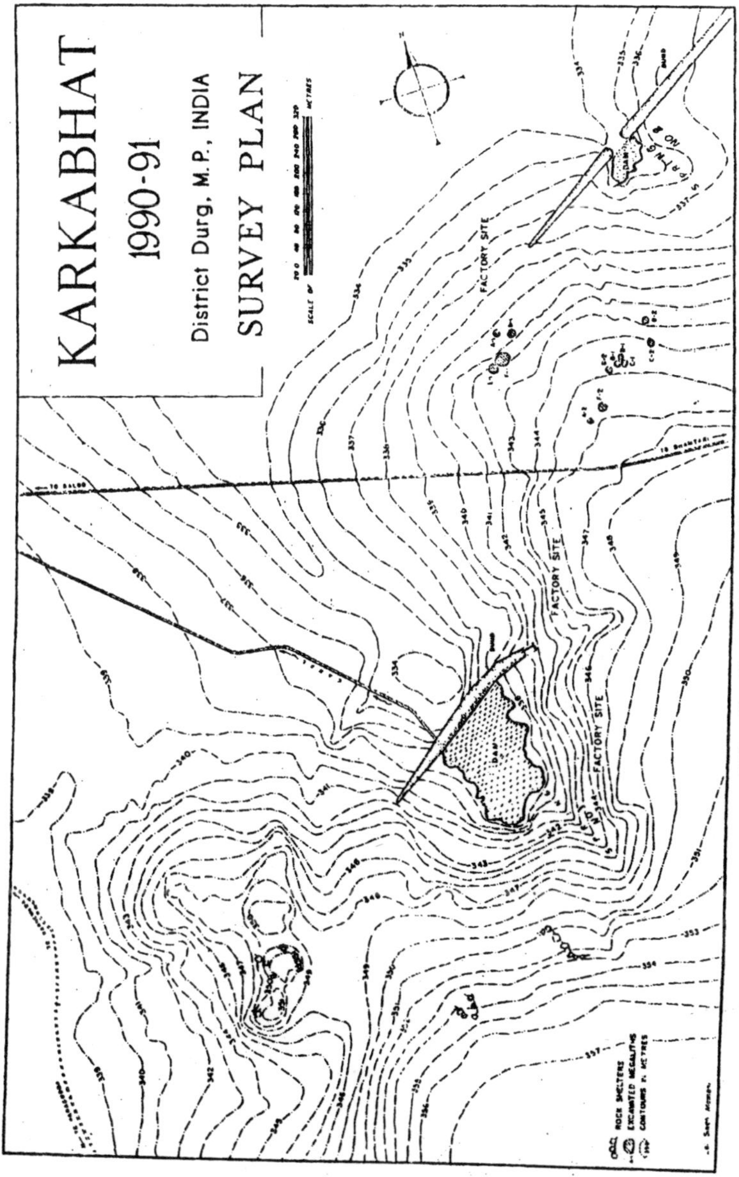

Fig. 2 : Karkabhat - Survey Plan

3

THE SITE

The sprawling megalithic site of Karkabhat is located in an approximate area of 10 sq. km. encompassing the villages of Karhi Badar, Kanyawada, Muzhgahan, Sorar, Chirchari, Tengna, Nahanda and Karkabhat. The entire area is dotted by natural springs and minor nallahs.All the megaliths are located on the rocky outcrops and high areas. The rock shelters are dotted on the peaks of the boldery outcrops. Karkabhat (Lat. 20°41'18"., Long. 81°19'7") is located 16 kms. from Balod on Balod-Dhamtari road. The site is spread over on both the sides of the road. As per our assessment, there must have been nearly 3500 to 4000 megalithic burials in this area, major part of which have now been totally wiped out. At Karkabhat itself there were more than 800 such burials.

At Karkabhat the Megalithic memorials of seven identified types are densely concentrated near the two perennial springs. (Fig. 2). They are located in the high rock bench and thin soil cover area, in a monsoon-fed lateritic zone, with the added advantage of having a large number of low natural rock shelters nearby. In the same area there are sprawling outcrops of trap and sandstone, where Menhirs of different sizes and shapes are still lying in finished and unfinished condition. Apart from these geological and topographic consideration location of megaliths at Karkabhat also appear to be influenced by the availability of iron, copper and gold. Iron ore deposits are confined to Dalli-Rajhara range of hills which are located nearly 20 kms. from Karkabhat. There are reserves in Dondi-Lohara also. Due to presence of several springs in the neighbourhood iron ore is available in very pure form.

Encrustation of copper have been found near Chicholi and Warar-Band, not very far from the site.

The site could easily be divided into three localities, e.g. (A) The Habitation, (B) The Factory Area and (C) The Megalithic Memorials Area. It is for the first time in the Indian sub-continent that all the three have been located at one particular site, adjacent to each other. Only few habitational areas of the megalithic period have been located and excavated extensively so far.

(A) Habitation

In Karkabhat-Sorar area two habitational areas, each of a different type could be located. Both are in the vicinity of one natural spring each. The rock shelters are to the south of spring No.1, whereas the open habitational area is to the north of spring No.2. In between the two springs lie the factory area and the burial area, with factory area to the north of spring No. 1.

a) Low rock shelters (Pls. III A & B)

To the south and south-west of the megalithic area on the southern bank of a natural spring there are a number of low rock shelters on a slowly rising granitic outcrops. The length and width of these rock shelters vary from 3 m to 2.5m, 1 m to 2m respectively. Each shelter has sufficient space to accommodate at least two persons during night and inclement weather conditions. As most of them open twoards north and north-east, they are well protected from south to south-east which is the normal direction of Mansoon showers. Due to constant use, the floors of these shelters have become smooth, gaining a sort of polish. This clearly indicates that they were under constant use. The question may be asked as to how they could be said to have been used by megalithic people. As microlithic tools are also found near the springs,

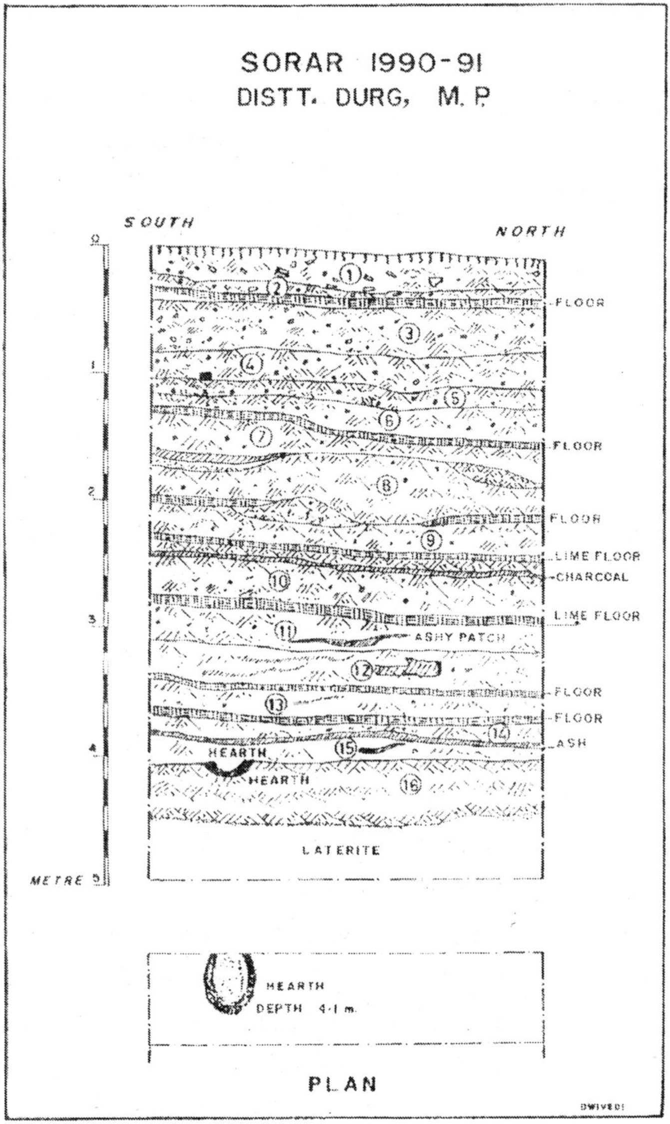

Fig. 3 : Sorar - Section facing west

it is likely that they were under use right from late Stone Age times.

b) The open habitational area (Fig 3, Pls. IV, V)

To the north of spring No. 2 is located village Sorar (20°40' N., 80°20' E). From the historical times the village is well known.[1] It still boasts of a ruined temple and a number of sculptures. But most important point that escaped the eyes of early investigators and historians are the two extensive mounds rising to the height of nearly 4.50 m. The probable cause of its non detection appears to be the present village lying right over these mounds. Plenty of potsherds dating back from megalithic period to historical period lie scattered all over the two mounds. It is the occurance of fine Black-and-Red ware that attracted our attention and gave the clue that probably a vast habitation of megalithic times lies buried under these mounds.

Due to lack of time and as our original plan was to excavate the megalithic burials only, only a small trench 3m x 3m could be laid for probing the deposit. The area selected was in the Middle School compound where there was enough open space to lay the trench. Moreover, this was the heighest poing available.

Black-and-Red ware (Fig 4), the typical megalithic pottery occurs right from layer 9 to layer 15, i.e. in a

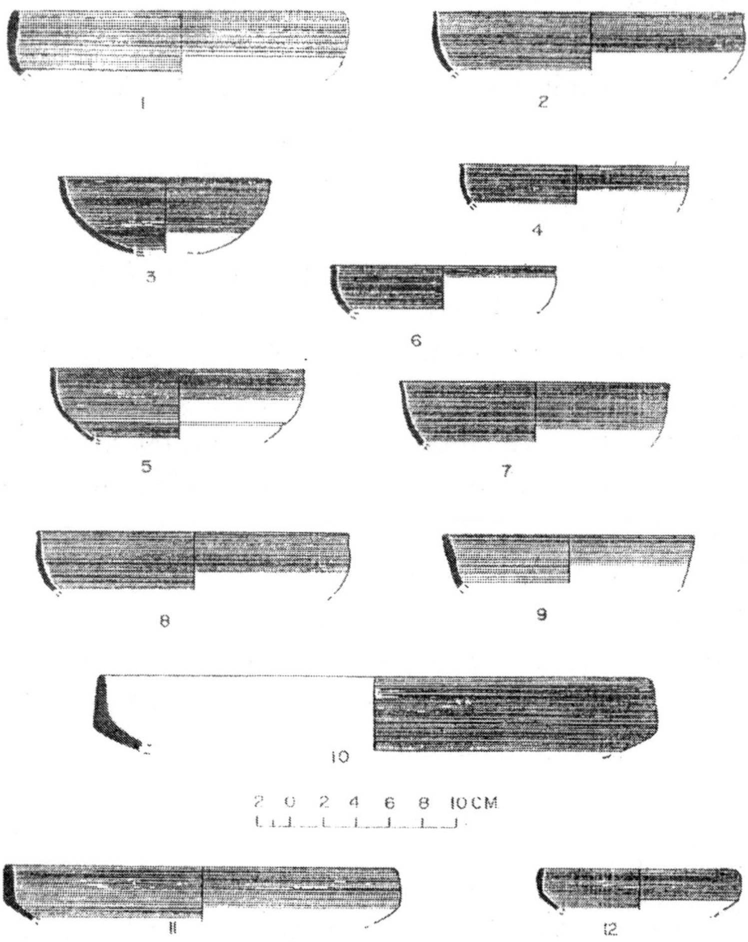

Fig. 4 : Sorar - Black-and-red ware from megalithic levels

total deposit of 2m. Almost each layer is sealed by a rammed mud or lime floor. Between layer 9 and 11 there are two lime floors of nearly 10 cms thick each. From layer 12 downwards mud floors ash layers and hearths are encountered. The first hearth in layer 15 appears right over the virigin soil of lateritic gravel. This 20cm thick layer is sealed by 5 cm thick deposit of ash. Right from layer 9 to layer 15 there is marked change in the composition of the deposits. While layers above 8 are made up of hard sticky clay mixed with yellowish soil and ash, the layers from 9 downwards are composed of loose soil, flor levels and plenty of ash deposits. Refuge pits cut through the floor levels also occur only from layer 9 downwards. These layers also yielded finer black-and-red ware pottery. From the meager nature of evidence, due to limited size of the area opened, it appears that the habitation of Black-and-Red period consisted of houses with rammed clay and lime floors in which wooden posts were sunk. The antiquities recovered from these layers (9 to 15) consist of iron, hop-scotches, mostly shaped out of potsherds and few stone objects like pestles.

Along with Black-and-Red wares, dull thick red ware and some painted sherds were also recovered from layer 10. Black burnished ware also occurs right from the lowest levels. In Black-and-Red ware the shapes that predominate are bowls and jars.

The stratigraphy described above is clear indication of megalithic levels. It could be safely surmised that the megalithic builders of Karkabhat lived in the spacious open area north of spring NO. 2. They constructed houses over wodden posts and have clean well rammed floors which were painted with red soil.

(B) The Factory Area (Pls. VIA &VB)

In between the two springs lies the factory site for cutting out and shaping menhirs of different sizes and shapes. Menhirs in various states of preparation could easily be seen lying all over the area. Advantage was taken of the thick deposit of uniform granitic outcrops, out of which it was easy to cut out and shape menhirs. Transportation of these huge blocks was easy to the adjoining burial area. It appears that for seperating huge blocks from the mother rock, first holes were created at regular intervals and probably boiling water was poured in these hole to develop cracks Once the derived size of the portion got seperated from the parent rock, it was easy to shape it according to the needs. Different sizes were required according to the status of the deceased. Different shapes were needed according to the month and time of demise of the deceased persons.

Fig. 5 : Karkabhat - Megalithic types-Distribution pattern

(C) The Memorial Area (Fig. 5)

The memorial burial site is located north of the factory site and in between the two natural springs which were source of constant supply of water. Only at Karkabhat the total area of concentration in which menhirs with cairn circles are spread is 2500 sq.m. with 517 megaliths in good conditions. Apart from this, near the rock shelters also, there are a number of menhirs and cairn circles.

On the basis of morphological features of menhirs and their layout seven types hae been identified. They are three more than identified earlier (I.A.R., 1956-57) at a nearby site of Dhanora excavated by Dr. M.G. Dikshit. The site has since been wiped out. The types identified and their numbers in the area of concentration are :

Type A - Stone cairn circle with loose packing, rising to a height of about 0.35 m from the ground level. 93-Area of each = 40 to 80 sq.m. (Pl. VII).

Type B- Stone cairn circle with distinct cairn heap rising upto a height of 1 to 1.30 m from the ground level. 88 - Area of each = 100 to 150sq.m. (Pl. VIII).

Type C - Stone cairn circle with a single manhir, small or big, in the centre of the circle and surrounded with heaped cairn packing. 134-Area of each=130 to 160 sq.m. (Pl. IX).

Type D- Stone cairn circle with two menhirs erected side by side in the northern half of the circle and surrounded with heaped cairn packing. 17 - Area of each = 167 sq.m. (Pl. X).

Type E-Stone cairn circle with two menhirs, are kept in the northern half and the other in the southern half of the circle, surrounded with heaped cairn packing. 79 - Area of each = 215 sq.m. (Pl. XI).

Type F- Stone cairn circle with multiple menhirs of varying sizes kept in two rows, one in the northern half and the other row in the southern half of the circle. All the menhirs are surrounded with heaped cairn packing. 39- Area of each = 30 to 150 sq.m. (Pl. XII).

Type G- Stone cairn circle with cap-stone in the centre resting over a heap of stones. Cap stone is oriented in north-south direction lengthwise. 67-Area of each = 67 to 100 sq.m. (Pl. XIII).

Reference

1. Beglar J.D., op.cit., p. 137-138, 142.

4

THE CUTTINGS

Twelve megalths of different types were excavated in order to ascertain their sepulchral nature and to find out the difference between each type. The evidence obtained from excavations clearly show that these menhirs and cairn circles are not associated with any sepulchral rite. They are only commemorative in nature.[1] Such a description finds mention in Tamil Sangam literature and ancient Tamil grammar *Tolkappiyam* as a stone commemorating a deceased warrior. They are almost invariably of granite or gneiss. At Karkabhat they have been raised in shallow pits and were propped up all round by a ring of rubble packing. The details of the excavated ones are as follows :

1. Type A

A cairn circle of loosely arranged rubbles covering an

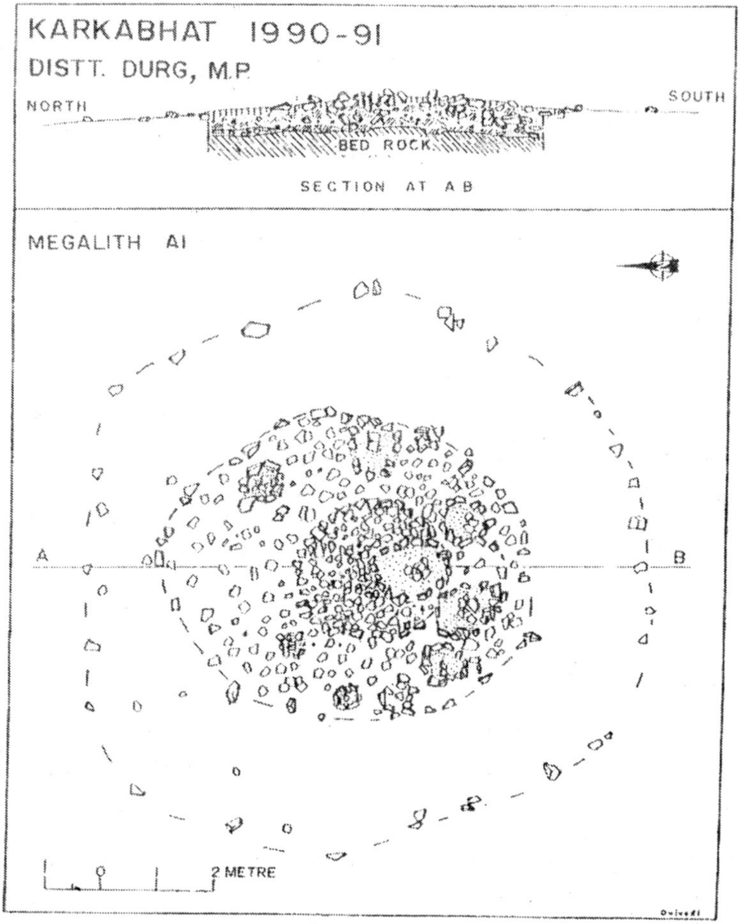

Fig. 6 : Plan and Section - Megalith A1

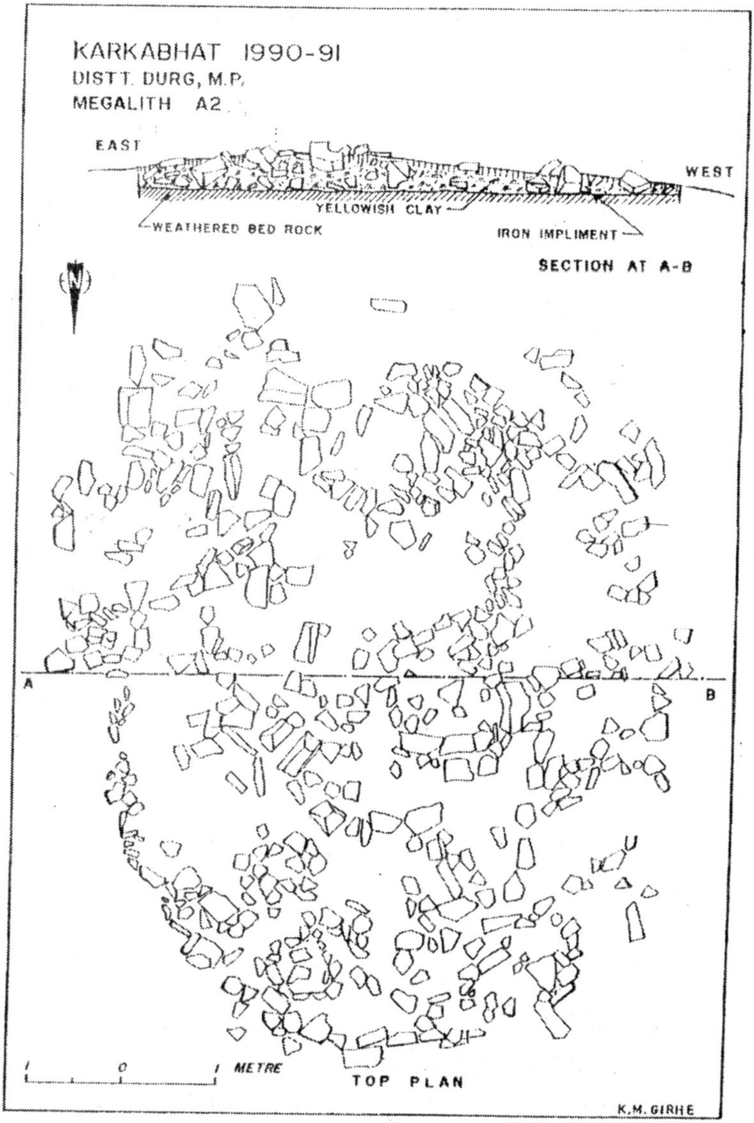

Fig. 7 : Plan and Section - Megalith A2

area varying from 45 to 81 sq.m. was created. From the ground level the cairn heap slowly rises in the pyramidical fashion. The rubbles are arranged in the form of small circles where each stone of the circle helps to form another circle. The height of the cairn heap varies from 0.40 to 0.60 m.

MEG. A1-(Fig 6, Pl. XIV)

Area of the	Cairn Circle	-	81 sq.m.
Diameter	NS	-	10 metres
	EW	-	10.25 "
Height of Cairn heap		-	0.60 "
Area excaated		-	32.00 "

(All four quadrants were excavated)

Apart from the rubbles the nature of filling comprises of fine yellowish clay. It is evident that the clay filling was also done in stages. The clay filling was thickest in the centre. No antiquity was recovered from this cairn circle.

MEG. A2 - (Fig. 7, Pl. XV)

Area of Cairn Circle		-	46 Sq.m.
Diameter	NS	-	8.00Metres
	EW	-	6.50"
Height of Cairn heap		-	0.15"
Area excavated		-	23.00 "
Maximum height of the section		-	0.40 "

Here also the filling comprised of yellowish fine clay. From Quadrant 1 a small silver ring was recovered. From level 3 in Quadrant 3 an iron spearhead lying just over the bed rock was recovered. (Pl. XXVI B)

2. Type B

MEG. B1-(Fig 8, Pl.XVI)

Area of the Cairn Circle	-	96 sq.m.
Diameter NS	-	12metres
EW	-	10"
Height of the cairn heap above G.L.	-	0.50"
Area excavated	-	48 sq.m.
Maximum height of the section	-	0.90 "

Along with the boulders the filling consitsted of yellowish loose earth. No antiquity was found from this megalith.

MEG. B2 - (Fig 9, PL. XVII)

Area of the Cairn Circle	-	157.5 sq.m.
Diameter NS	-	14.50metres
EW	-	12.50"
Height of thhe Cairn heap above G.L.	-	0.45 "
Area excavated	-	128.5 "

The filling consists of yellowish fine earth along with the boulders. Just above the weathered bed rock

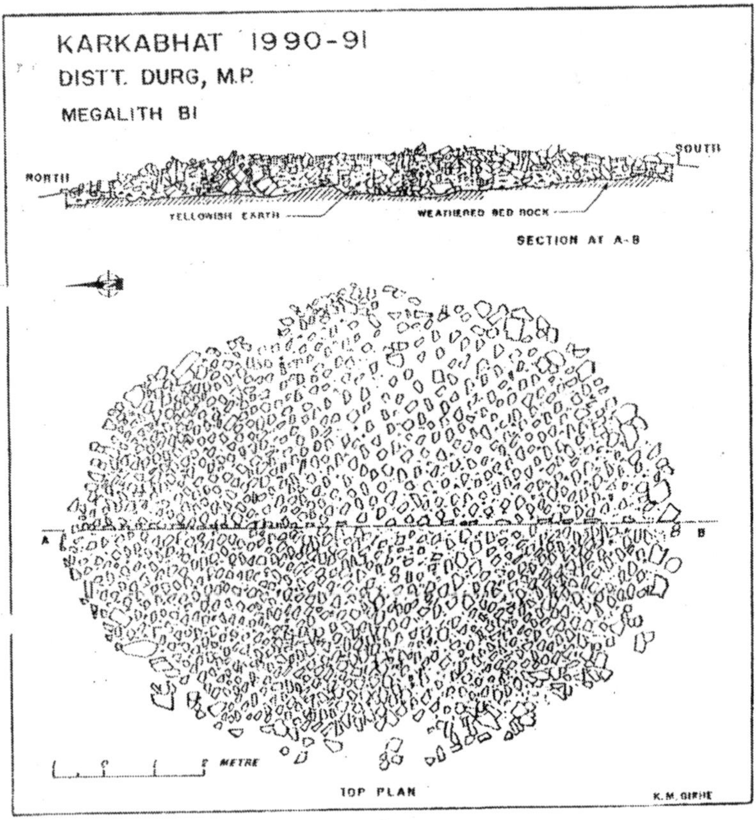

Fig. 8 : Plan and Section - Megalith B1

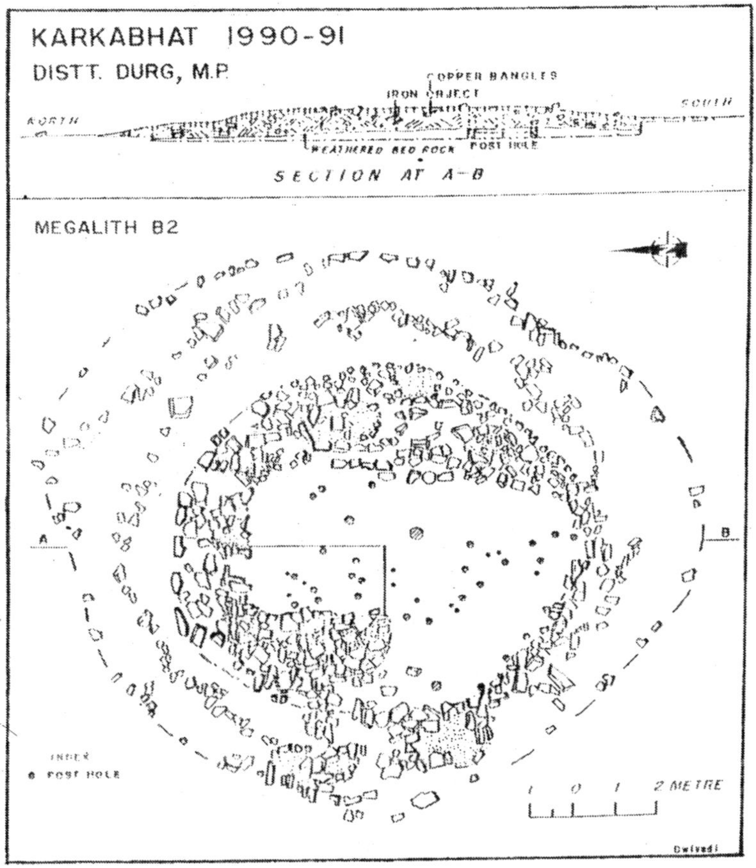

Fig. 9 : Plan and Section - Megalith B2

number of post-holes were located in the central portion of the circle. In this case the cairn circle appears to have been enlarged subsequently as two distinct linings of more than the normal size boulders used for filling were present. From the alignment of the post holes it appears that before coming up of the cairn heap some structure resting over wooden poles existed.

From level 2 of Quadrant 3 four copper bangles and one soft stone barrel bead, was recovered. From level 4 of the same quadrant one iron spearhead and one spike were recovered. (Pl. XXVIB).

3. MEG. C1 - (Fig. 10, Pl. XVIII)

Area of the circle	-	130 sq.m.
Diameter NS	-	14metre
EW	-	13 "
Height of Cairn heap	-	0.30"
Height of Menhir above G.L.	-	2.75"
Width of Menhir	-	1.30"
Thickness of Menhir	-	0.40"
Area excavated	-	65sq.m.
Height of Section	-	1.0 metre

The menhir is roughly 'Y' shaped, i.e. forked on the top. This was one of the earliest to be photographed.[2] Along with the boulders the filling consisted of yellowish loose clay. Only the northern half of the circle was excavated upto bed rock. No antiquity was recovered from this megalith.

MEG. C2 - (Fig 11, Pl. XIX)

Area of the Circle	-	158sq.m.
Diameter NS	-	18 metre
EW	-	13"
Height of the Cairn heap above G.L.	-	0.75"
Height of Menhir above G.L.	-	1.05"
Width	-	0.60"
Area excavated	-	140.00 sq.m.

The filling consisted of yellowish compact clay along with boulders. Unlike in other cases the centre did not have much filling. The menhir was found in fallen condition. It appears that for the purpose of making road ballast the menhir was pulled down after removing the filling around it.

From level 3 of Quadrant 3 highly coroded iron dagger was recovered.

4. MEG. D1 - (Fig. 12, Pl. XX)

Area of Cairn circle	-	167 sq.m.
Diameter NS	-	14.80 metre
EW	-	15.00"
Menhir (east) Length	-	2.45"
Width	-	0.92"
Menhir (West) Length	-	2.25"

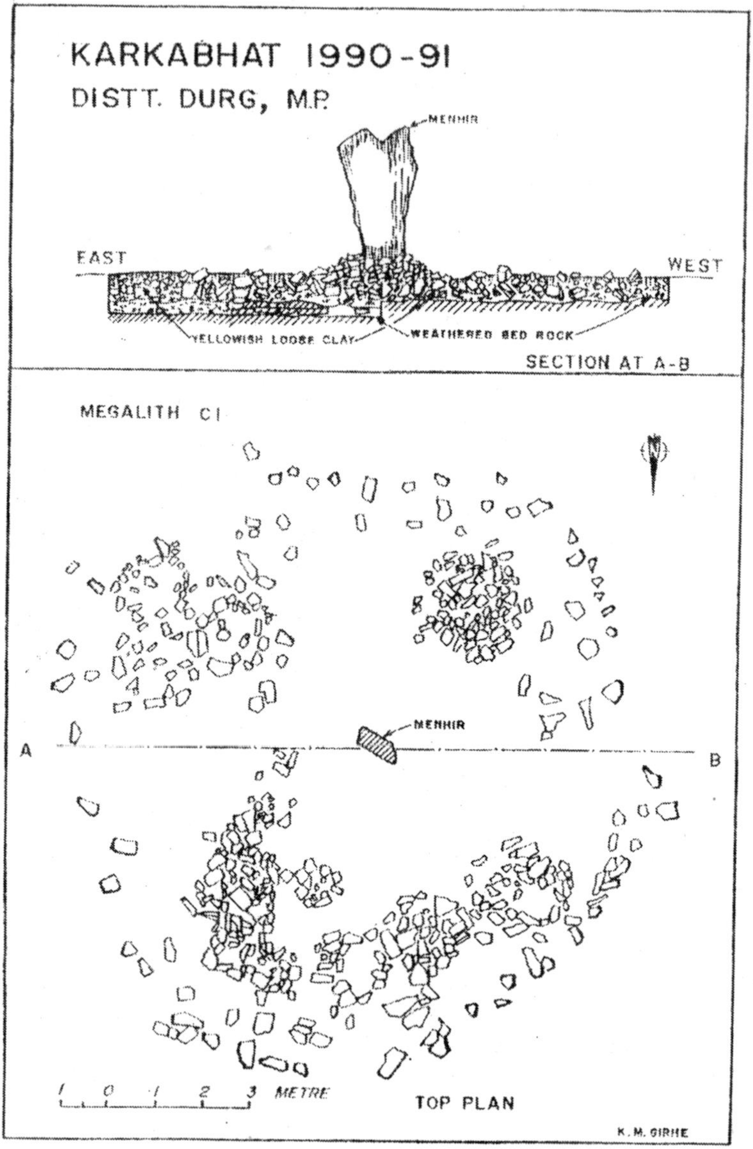

Fig. 10 : Plan and Section - Megalith C1

(Broken & fallen)	Width	-	0.92"
Height of the	Menhir	-	2.40"
Area excavated		-	92 sq.m.

The western menhir was erected and filling of cairn pebbles was done right over the bed rock, whereas the eastern menhir was erected a little latter as indicated by the pit line. The southeastern quadrant yielded an iron plough share from the lowest level. (Pl. XXVII B).

It appears that the two menhirs were erected in memory of two individuals who were closely related may be husband and wife. The western menhir lies broken. Only two diagonal quadrants were excavated.

5. MEG. E1 - (Fig 13. Pl. XXI)

Area of Cairn Circle		-	216 sq.m.
Diameter	NS	-	20 metre
	EW	-	15"
Maximum height of Cairn heap above G.L.		-	1.20"
Menhirs			
Northern	Length	-	2.00"
	Width	-	0.60"
	Thickness	-	0.50"
Southern	Length	-	1.40"
	Width	-	0.80"
	Thickness	-	0.25"

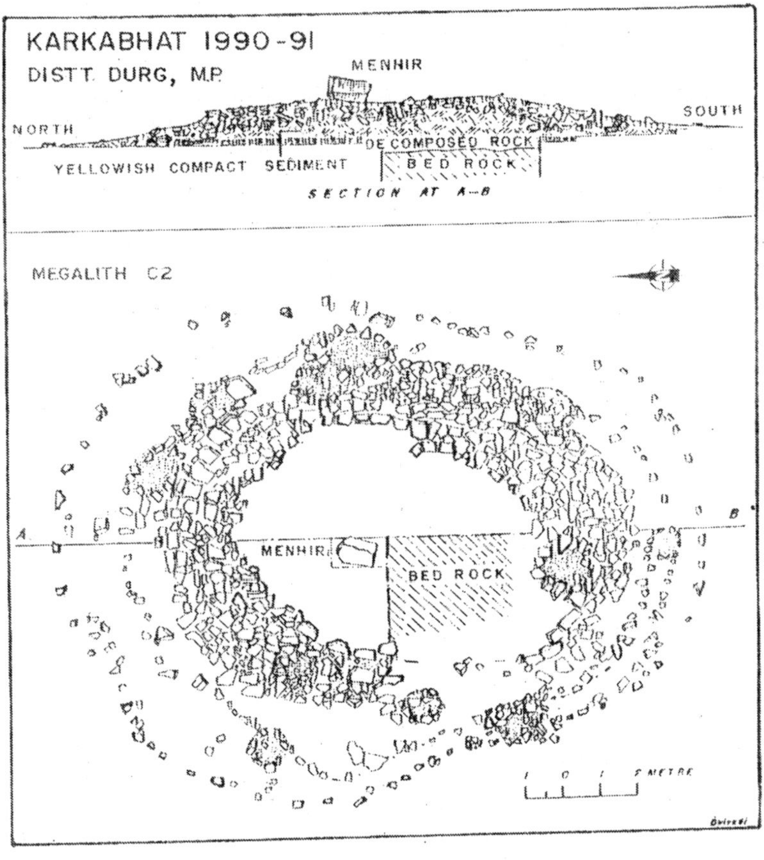

Fig. 11 : Plan and Section - Megalith C2

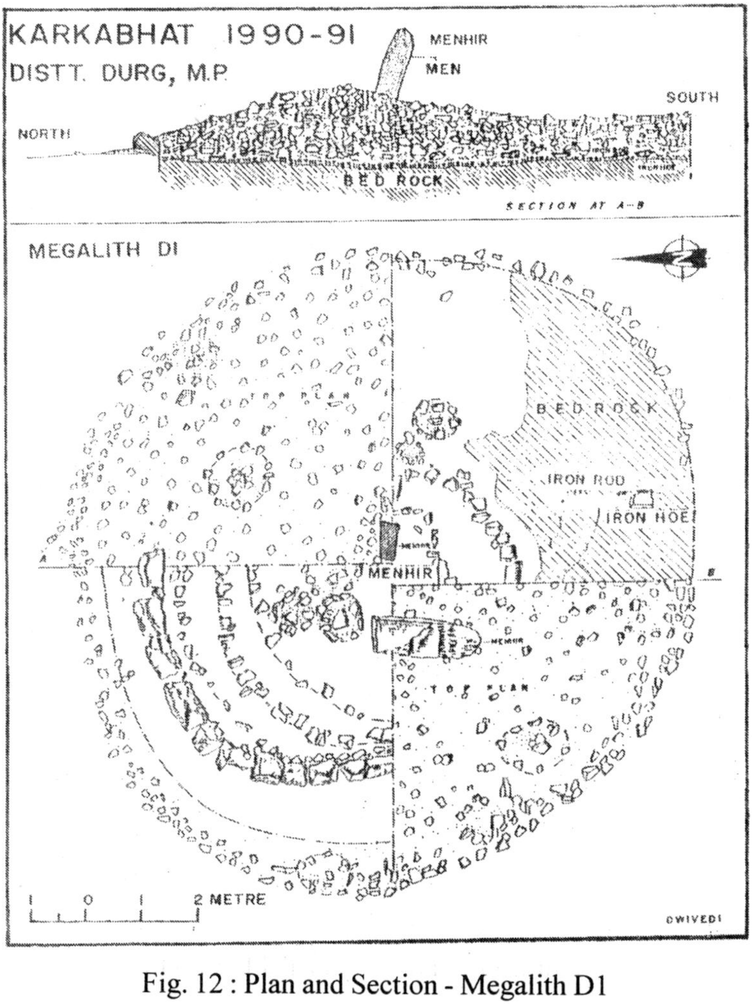

Fig. 12 : Plan and Section - Megalith D1

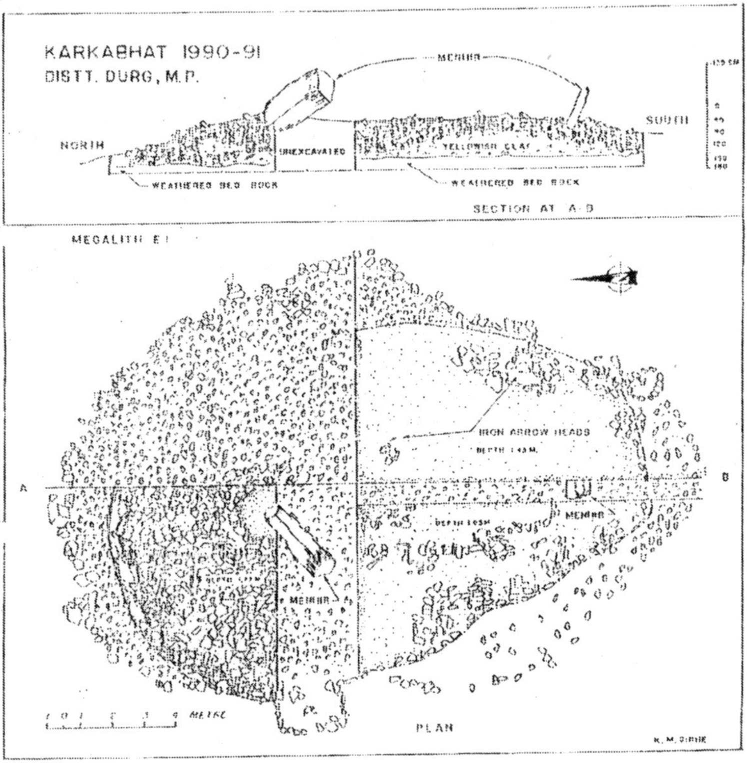

Fig. 13 : Plan and Section - Megalith E1

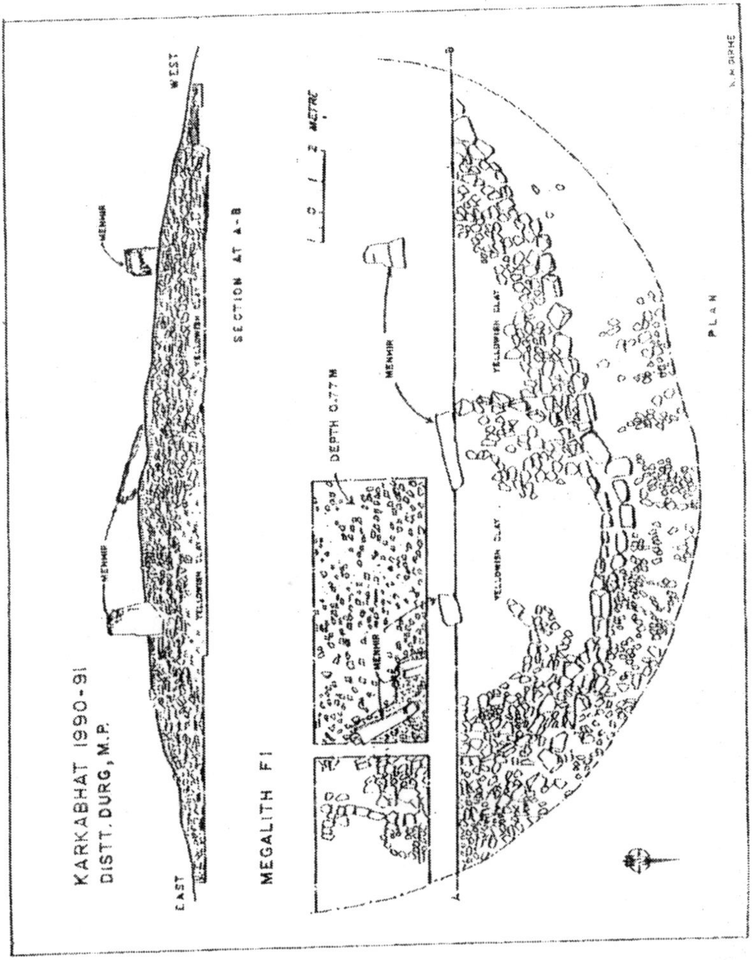

Fig. 14 : Plan and Section - Megalith F1

Area excavated	-	162 sq.m.
Maximum height of Section	-	2.00 metre

The cairn was oblong in shape. Two diagonal quadrants were excavated. Three iron arrow heads, two in good shape, were recovered from level 5 of Quardant 2. One of them was found from inside the small stone circle near the south-eastern corner of the outer circle. (Pl. XXVIII A).

The filling in this case consisted of pebbles mixed with red lateritic silt, unlike in earlier referred to types where it was fine yellow clay.

6. MEG. F1 - (Fig. 14, Pl. XXII)

(The group of family memorials)

In this megalithic cairn heap there are eleven menhirs of different sizes, five in the northern side and six in the southern side. This is one of the largest cairn heap and circle of its type at Karkabhat. In order to understand the significance of erecting so many menhirs in one cairn heap northern half of the cairn heap was subjected to investigation.

Area of the cairn circle		-	627 sq.m.
Maximum height of cairn heap		-	1.80 metre
Diameter	EW	-	32"
	NS	-	24"

Menhir 1	Height	-	1.90 "
	Width	-	1.10"
	Thickness	-	0.60"
Menhir 2	Height	-	2.60"
	Width	-	0.80"
	Thickness	-	0.50
Menhir 3	Height	-	1.40 "
	Width	-	1.00"
	Thickness	-	0.60"

Measurements of only those menhirs on the northern side were taken that fell in the East-West section.

Area excavated - 227.25 sq.m.

Maximum height of section - 2.10 metre

The pit lines and filling of the above mentioned menhirs clearly show that they are erected at different times as each had a pit line of its own, with depth, varying, Menhir No. 1 was the first to be erected. The outer ring of the cairn heap, particularly on the northern side was lined with bigger than the size of boulders used for filling, as in all other cases. But in this type evidences show that double line of boulders was subsequently enlarged on east and west with the erection of more menhirs. This is the features which has been observed for the first time and speaks of the architectural skill of the Karkabhat megalithicians.

Just below Menhir No. 1, a 26 cm. long dagger was recovered from level 7 of quadrant 1. The offering

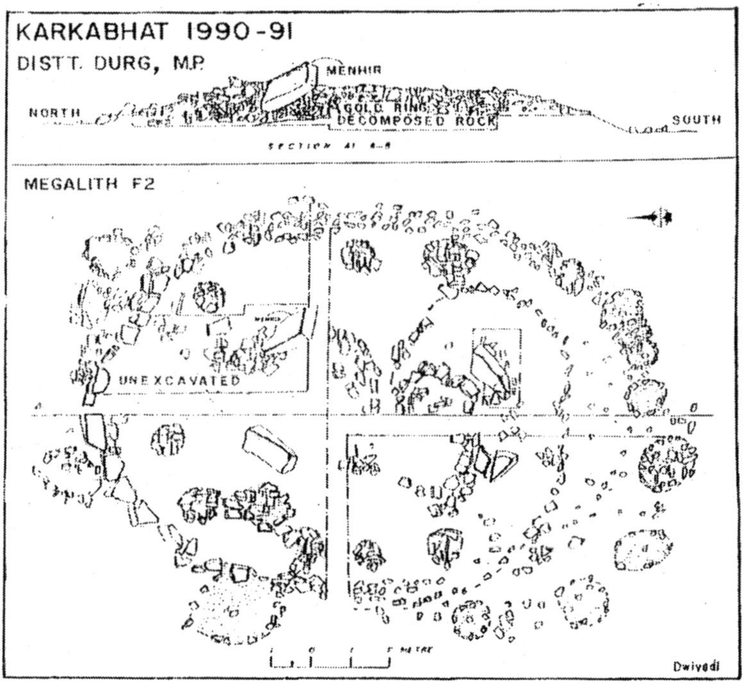

Fig. 15 : Plan and Section - Megalith F2

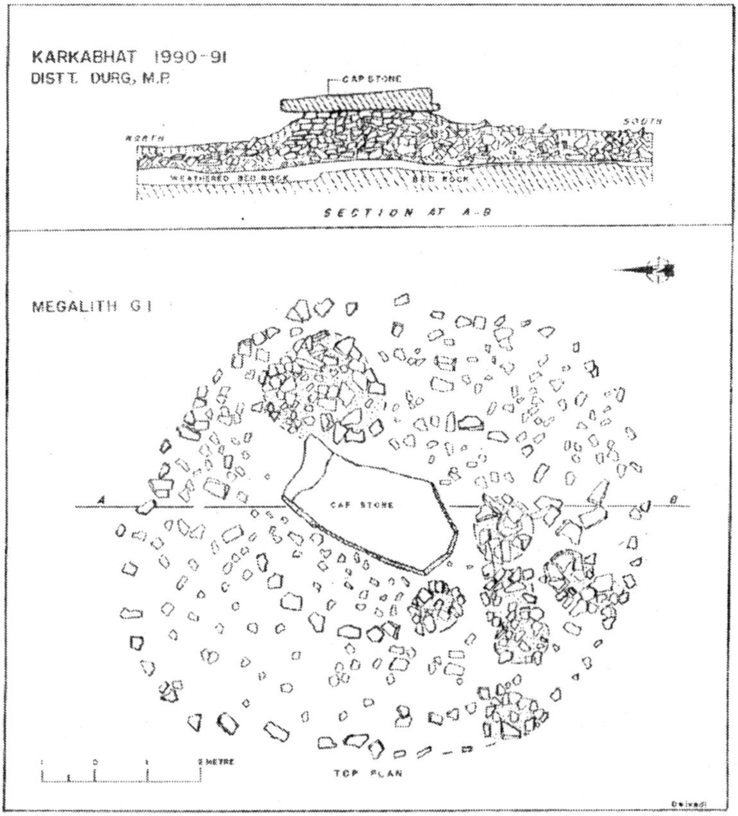

Fig. 16 : Plan and Section - Megalith G1

was kept in a small stone circle.

Unfortunately, due to lack of time the southern counterparts of the northern menhirs could not be excavated. This would have enabled us in understanding whether 'F' type of Megalith is a composite form of a number of 'E' type megaliths or it differs in any way from that type.

MEG. F2 - (Fig. 15, Pl. XXIII)

It is a case of compsite form of two E types of megaliths. There are four menhirs, two in the north and two in the south.

Area of Cairn heap		-	148.5 metre
Diameter	NS	-	15.40"
	EW	-	10.34"
Maximum height of cairn heap		-	0.93"
Area excavated		-	128.sq.m.

The sections across north-south clearly shows that the menhirs of each group, i.e. north and south were erected at the same time as their pit and filling levels were same. But there appears to be time gap between both the groups. Out of the two groups, one may belong to husband and the other to the wife. Another interesting feature of this megalith was the occurance of small circles of stones, forming a garland around the outer periphery of the cairn circle.

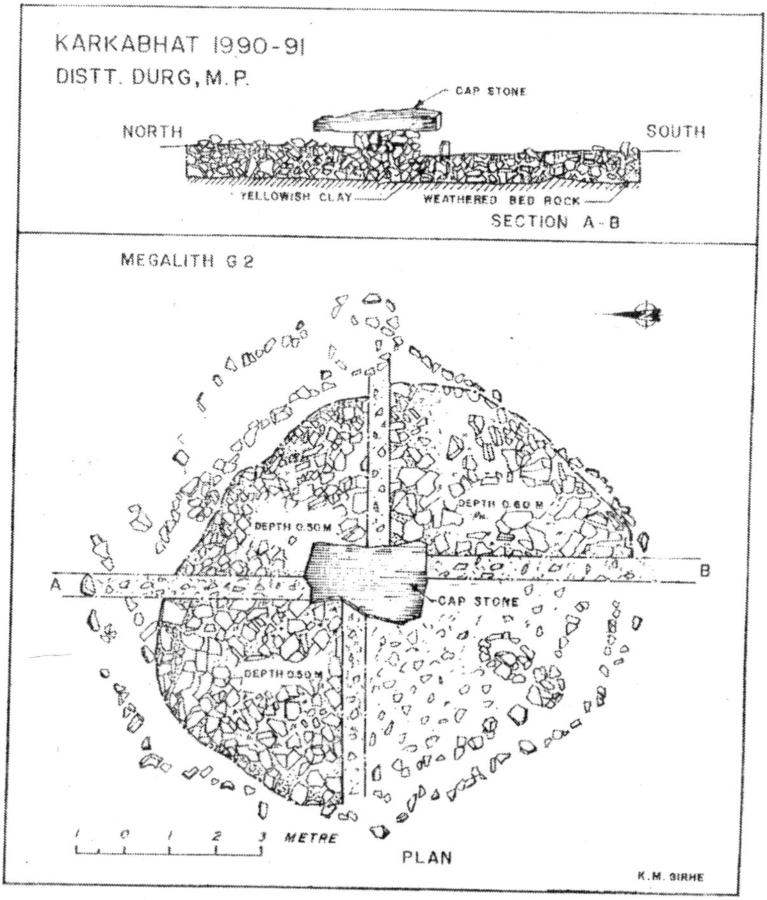

Fig, 17 : Plan and Section - Megalith G2

Two small gold rings, one of the wire type were recovered from the western group. Both were found in two separate small stone circles, resting just over the bed rock. (Pl. XXVIII B).

7. MEG. G1 - (Fig. 16, Pl. XXIV)

The capstone oriented norht-south rests in the centre over the heap of cairn, leaving rest of the capstone free.The broader end of the capstone is towards south whereas the narrower towards north.

Area of the Cairn circle		-	69 sq.m.
Diameter	NS	-	9.10 metre
	EW	-	8.25 "
Maximum height of cairn heap		-	0.72"
Length of capstone		-	3.10 "
Width of the capstone		-	1.95"
Area excavated		-	69 sq.m.

A number of small stone circles were noticed in the entire circle at different levels. No offerings were recovered from this megalith.

MEG. G2 - (Fig. 17, Pl. XXV)

Area of cairn circle	-	100 sq.m.
Maximum height of cairn heap above G.L.	-	0.30 metre
Length of capstone	-	2.70"
Width of capstone	-	1.70"

Thickness of capstone - 0.25"
Area excavated -
Maximum height of Section - 0.60metre
No antiquity was recovered from the dig.

References

1. Thapar B.K., Maski 1954: *A Chalcolithic site of the Southern Deccan in Ancient India No. 13*, Delhi, 1957, p. 35.
2. *A.S.I. Annual Report*, 1930-34, Part II, Pl. LXXVII (b).

5

FINDS

I Iron objects

Antiquitywise Karkabhat memorial burials are not very rich. It is understandable as the menhirs were erected and cairn heaps raised around them only as memorials and minimum ritualistic offerings were made, probably according to the status of the deceased. Amongst the metallic objects interned, iron objects are largest in number. It is evident, with the source of iron ore plenty in the area, the megalithic people of the area had the knowledge of indigenous smelting technology. Even to day the tribals of the adjoining Bastar area and the 'Agharias' in District Durg, smelt their own iron for their use which is of high quality.

In all seventeen iron objects were recovered from the excavations. They could be conveiently divided into two main categories -

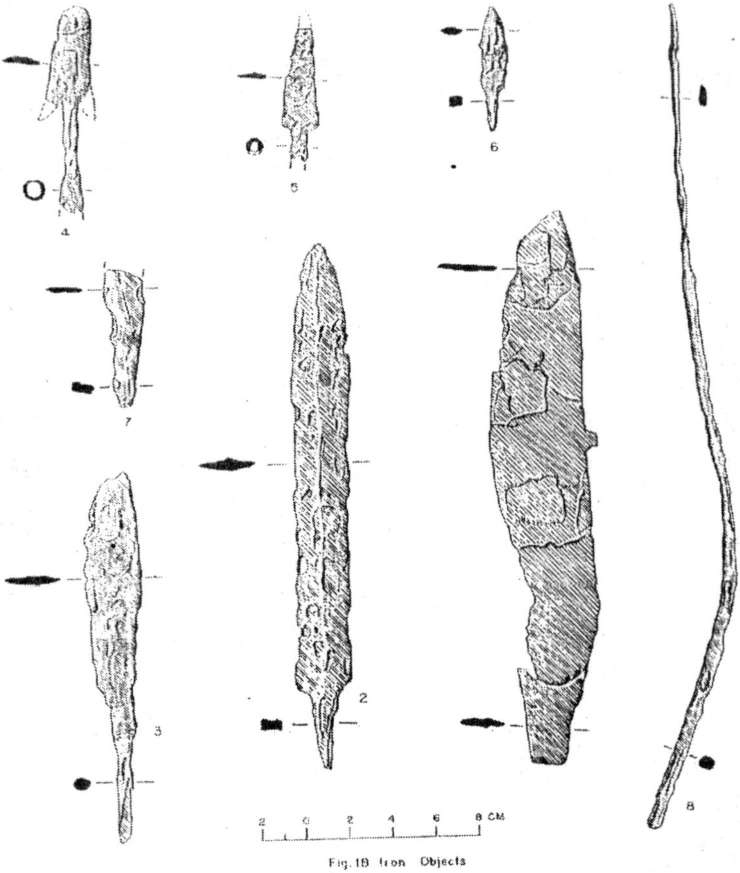

Fig. 18 : Iron Objects

A) Objects of offence and
B) Objects of Agricultural and Domestic use
A) Objects of Offence (Fig. 18, Pl. XXVI A)

a) Dagger Blades

In the collection there are five of them, each slightly different from the other typologically.

Accession No. 10 : (Fig. 10, Pl. XVI A, 2).

The incomplete object was recovered from the third level of Quadrant 3 of Megalith C2. The implement is in a highly corroded state, fragile and at places flaked off. It measures 27.5 cm. in length, 5 cm in width and 5 cm in thickness. It is divided into two parts, blade and tang. The blade is plano-convex and transverse in cross section. The rectangular tang is 4.8 cm in length.

Accession No. 24 : (Pl. XXVI A, 3)

From Megalith F1, Quadrant 1, Level VII.

It is comparatively in a better state of preservation, measuring 26 cm in length, 2.7 cm in width and 0.6 cm in thickness. The blade is lanceolated having mid-rib. Both the edges of the blade are straight, tapering towards free ends ultimately converging into a sharp point. The solid tang narrows towards the hafting end. It is rectangular in shape and cross section.

This type is very common and has been reported from Megalithic sites of Vidarbha region and South India, viz. Naikund,[1] Khapa-Gangapur,[2] Nagarjunakonda,[3] Satanikota,[4] Brahmagiri,[5] Parkalam[6] and Sanur.[7]

Accession No. 11: (Pl. XXVI A, 4)

From Megalith D1, Quadrant 2, Level IX.

The weapon is highly rusted, fragile and broken at the distal end of the blade. It measures 18.5 cm in length, 2.7 cm in width, and 0.5 cm in thickness. Blade is lanceolated. Both the convex edges converge towards both the ends. It is transverse in cross section. It has 4.8 cm long tang with a mid-rib. The tang is flaring towards the free end and is trucated. It has a lanticular cross section.

Similar types of daggers have been reported from Satanikota.[8]

Accession No. 2: (Pl. XXVI A, 1)

From Megalith A2, Quadrant 3, Level III.

It is a very long specimen with a socketed end, possibly a sword. Rusted, fragile and broken into seven parts, measures 20 cm in length, 3.3 cm in width and 0.5 cm in thickness. It is rectangular in shape and transverse in cross-section. It had an oblique tip. It has a circular handle which is broken. It is hollow from inside.

Such types of long daggers or swords have been reported from Brahmgiri[9] and Sanur.[10]

Accession No. 15 :

From Megalith F1, Quadrant 1, Level V.

The weapon is in highly corroded and fragile condition. Lower part is missing. Transverse in cross section and rectangular in shape, it has a straight tip. It measures 13 cm in length, 3.7 cm in width and 1.1 cm in thickness.

Similar weapon is reported from Nagarjunakonda.[1]

b) Arrow Heads (Fig. 20, Pl. XXIX A)

In all four arrow heads all of different types have been recovered from the excavation.

Accession No. 22 : (Pl. XXIX A, 1)

From Megalith E1, Quadrant 2, Level V.

Heavily corroded. Measures 10 cm in length, 2.3 cm in width and 0.4 cm in thickness. The weapon consists of a pointed barbed blade and a tang. The left lower end of the blade is barbed. The point is rectangular in shape and biconvex in cross section. The tang is longer than the blade, circular in cross section and widens at the basal end for hafting.

Such type of arrow heads have been reported from the Megaliths of Takalghat[12] and Sanur.[13]

Accession No. 23 : (Pl. XXIX A, 3)

From Megalith E1, Quadrant 2, Level V.

The weapon measures 6.7 cm in length, 1.8 cm in width and 0.5 cm in thickness. It has a leaf shaped, biconvex point. The straight tip is missing, the tang is very short, hollow and broken at the lower end, It is plano-convex in cross section.

Similar type have been reported from the Megaliths of Takalghat, Kapa[14] and Sanur.[15]

Accession No. 19 : (XXIX A, 2).

From Megalith E1, Quadrant 2, Level V.

Highly corroded and broken on left half. Measures 6.3 cm in length, 1.3 cm in width and 0.3 cm in thickness. The point is leaf-shaped having bi-convex cross section and pointed tip. The tang is short and retangular with a pointed lower end.

This type of arrow heads have been reported from Takalghat, Khapa[16] and Sanur[17].

Accession No. 20: (Pl. XXIX A, 4)

From Megalith E1, Quadrant 3, Level V.

The point of this tangless arrow head is leaf-shaped with truncated tip and oblique lower end. In cross section it is bi-convex. It measures 6.8 cm in length, 2 cm in width and 0.5 cm in thickness.

c) Spikes

Accession No. 13 : (Pl. XXIX B, 2)

From Megalith B2, Quadrant 3.

Only blade portion has been recovered from the excavation. The blade is hollow with a pointed tip. The tang portion is missing. It measures 11.2 cm in length, 1.6 cm in diameter and 1.4 cm in thickness.

Similar objects have been reported from khapa and Gangapur[18] megalithic stone circles.

Accession No. 25: (Pl. XXIX B, 1)

From Megalith F1, Quadrant 1, Level VII.

The object was found in two pieces. It has a long tang and a short blade. The blade is thinner than the tang and tapers towards the tip which is pointed. Blade and tang, both are rectangular in shape. The tang is twisted from the middle. The weapon measures 41 cm in length, 1 cm in width and 0.7 cm in thickness.

Such spikes have been reported from Khapa[19], Brahmagiri[20] and Sanur.[21]

d) Spearhead

Accession No. 12 : (Pl. XXIX B, 3)

The long spread head from the excavations at Karkabhat was recovered from Megalith B2, Quadrant 3. It is heavily rusted, broken and fragile. It has a rectangular blade with broken tip. It is bi-convex in section. The hallow tang is cylindrical in shape, wider at the lower end with a mid-rib. The weapon measures 17.7 cm in length, 21 cm in width and 1.7 cm in thickness.

B) Agricultural Implement (Pl. XXX A)

Accession No. 21 :

The long implement was recovered from Quadrant 2, Level VIII ov Megalith D1, Due to heavy encrustation it was recovered in serval pieces. It was found near the outer ring of the cairn circle, Just over the bed rock. It is crescentic in shape and bifurcated. The curved ends make sharp cutting edges on the lower side.

It is a fine example of a plough share. The curved upper part was for hafting. A similar plough-share has been reported from Ramapuram[22], where it has been dated to around the beginning of the first millenium B.C.

Similar find at Karkabhat clearly takes back the antiquity of megaliths to the above mentioned dates.

II. Copper Objects (Fig. 19, Pl. XXX B)

Compared to iron objects, the number of copper objects are less. They comprise only nearly 25% of the iron objects. Only 4 bangles were recovered and that too all from Level II of quadrant 3 of Megalith B2. This megalith also yielded a stone bead along with the bangles from the same spot. From Level IV two iron objects were also recovered. The bangles were found in groups of two each. Two of them are of (i) ends meeting types whereas one is of (ii) 'open ends' type and the fourth is (iii) with overlapping ends.

Accession No. 6 : (Fig. 19, Pl. XXXB, 2)

i) Ends meeting type

Outer diameter - 5.02cm

Inner diameter - 4.03"

Accession No. 5 : (Fig 19, Pl. XXX B, 1)

Outer diameter - 6.00 cm

Inner diameter - 5.04 cm

In this case also the meeting ends are thicker and bulbous.

Accession No. 7 : (Fig. 19, Pl. XXX B, 3)

ii) Open ends type

Outer diameter - 5.04 cm

Inner diameter - 4.09 "

Accession No. 4 : (Fig. 19, Pl. XXX B, 4)

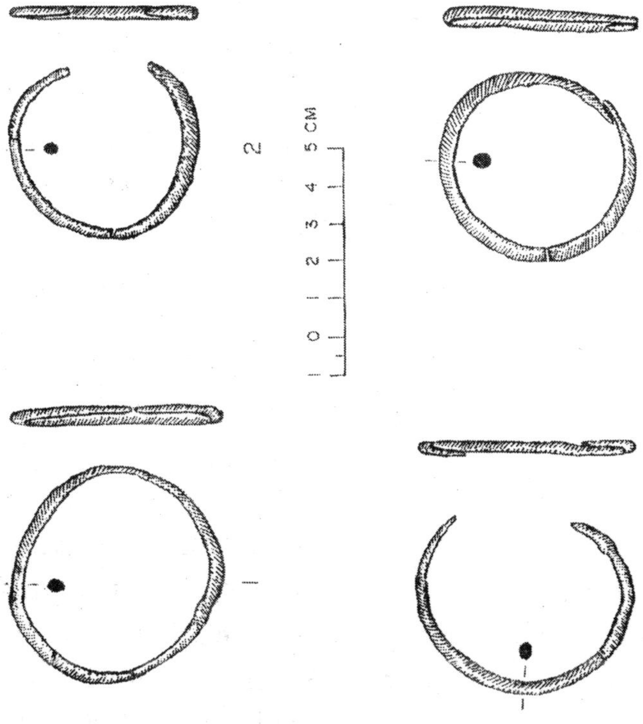

Fig. 19 : Copper Objects

iii) Overlapping ends type

Outer diameter - 5.03cm

Inner diameter - 4.06 "

Due to acidity in the soil, all the bangles are in very corroded and fragile state with plenty of copper sulphate formation.

III Gold objects (Pl. XXX B, 5, 6)

Only two gold objects, both rings, were found. Both were recovered from quadrant 3 of Megalith F2, but from different levels.

Accession No. 9 : (Pl. XXX B, 5)

It is thick wire ring, twice coiled, with open ends. It was recovered from Level III. The wire is circular in cross section. The rings outer diameter is 1.2 cm, whereas the inner diameter is 0.9 cm. It could have been used by a child or as ear ring by an adult.

Accession No. 14 : (Pl. XXX B, 6)

A double coiled thin wire ring, with cros section of wire circular, was recovered from Level IV. The wire is 6.2 cm long. The outer diameter of the ring is 1.0 cm whereas the inner diameter is 0.85 cm. One of the ends is pointed whereas the outer free ends has a cut mark. It is likely that the object waş used as a nose ring and the nose skin was pierced by the sharp pointed end. Even today the nose and ear piercing ceremony is observed in the area for children of both the sexes. It is an auspicious occasion which is celebrated with feast amongst the close relatives.

IV. Silver Object

Accession No. 1 : (Pl. XXX B, 8)

Only one small silver wire nose ring in three pieces, was recovered from the depth of 0.37 cm in quadrant 1 of Megalith A2. The outer diameter is 1.1 cm and inner diameter is 0.9 cm. The thickness of wire is 0.1 cm. It is closed ring.

V. Bead

Accession No. 8 : (Pl. XXX B, 7)

From the entire dig only one soapstone long barrel circular bead was found. Only half is present. It was recovered from the depth of 10 cm in Quadrant 3 of Megalith B2. From the same place of this megalith from copper bangles were recovered. The maximum available length is 2.2 cm. It has been well polished.

References

1. Deo, S.B., 1982, Naikund Excavation, Bombay, p. 35, Fig. 24-11.
2. Deo, S.B. 1970, Excavations at takalghat and Khapa, Nagpur, p. 46, pl. XII-6, Fig. 24-6.
3. Subrahmanyam, R., 1975, Nagarjunakonda, Calcutta, p. 181, Fig. 87-17.
4. Ghosh, N.C. 1986, Excavations at Satanikota, calcutta, p. 159, pl. LVI-5.

5. A.I. No. 4, 1948, Brahmagiri and Chandravalli, 1947, p. 257, Fig. 37-12.
6. A.I. No. 8, 1952, Parkalam 1948 : Excavation of a Megalithic Urn Burial, p. 16, Fig. 6-1.
7. A.I. No. 15, 1959, Sanur 1950 & 1952 : A Megalithic site in Distt. Chingleput, p. 35, Fig. 10-9.
8. Ghosh N.C., op.cit., p. 159, pl. LVI-3.
9. A.I. No. 4, 1948, Brahmagiri and Chandravalli, 1947, p. 260, Fig. 39-36.
10. A.I. No. 15, 1959, Sanur 1950 and 1952 : A megalithic site in Distt. Chingleput, p. 35, Fig. 10-6.
11. Dubrahmanyam, R., 1975, Nagarjunakonda, Calcutta, p. 181, Fig. 87-12, 21.
12. Deo, S.B., 1970, Exczvztions at Takalghat and Khapa, Nagpur, p. 46, Fig. 24-7.
13. A.I. No. 15, 1959, Sanur, 1950 and 1952 : A Megalithic site in Distt. Chingleput, p. 37, Fig. 11-19.
14. Deo, S.B., 1970, Excavations at Takalghat and Khapa, Nagpur, p. 47, pl. XII-8, Fig. 24-8.
15. A.I. No. 15, 1959, Sanur, 1950 and 1952; A Megalithic site in Distt. Chingleput, p. 37, Fig. 11-18.
16. Deo, S.B., 1970, Excavations at Takalghat and Khapa, Nagpur, p. 47, pl. XII-4, Fig. 24-4.
17. A.I. No. 15, 1959, Sanur, 1950 and 1952, A Megalithic site in Distt. Chingleput, p. 37, Fig. 11-23.
18. Deo, S.B., 1970, Excavations at Takalghat and Khapa, Nagpur, p. 47, pl. XII-1, Fig. 24-1.
19. Ibid., p.47, pl. XII-2, Fig. 24-2.
20. A.I. No. 4, 1948, Brahmagiri and Chandravalli, 1947, p. 254, Fig. 35-1.
21. A.I. No. 15, 1959, Sanur, 1950 and 1952, A Megalithic site in Distt. Chingleput, p. 35, Fig. 9-2.
22. Puratattva, No. 11, 1979-80, Protohistoric Indian Metal tools from villages - A Note, pp. 59-63.

6

ARCHITECTURE

Karkabhat Megalithic people had an advanced knowledge of sepulchral architecture, involving cutting, shaping, transporting and erecting such huge Menhirs as memorials. Even huge quantity of boulders were also transported and arranged around the Menhirs, meticulously. In case of multiple Menhir memorials involving two or more than two Menhirs care was taken to erect them at right place in the right direction and in case of multiple burials at equidistance. Each cairn circle was lined with big boulders in the northern half and then at the bottom level and distinct circle of stones was made. This circle was enlarged with great precision with the induction of more menhirs in course of time. Even in case of single menhir the suocessive layers of boulders were arranged in a pyramidical fashion slowly rising to the top. In each case right from the bottom the entire space around the Menhirs/capstones, was filled with boulders arranged in circles with a central stone. (Pl. XXXI). Each stone of the circle formed another circle, in this way a number of circles were created filling the whole area. After the creation of first stage of circles the entire area was filled with yellow or red fine silt. Over the filling the process of making circles was again repeated. This was done till the filling reached the desired height. Thus, number of circles from bottom to top in different state were created in a receeding fashion. It is not clear whether this process was continued in a regular manner withoug break in course of few days/months or was continued after breaks. The earlier possibility as per evidence appears to be more likely.

This method of raising the cairn height with circles and successive filling is a new feature observed. It is in one of these circles that the offerings were deposited.

Thus the Megalithic people of Karkabhat adopted the circles and pyramidical form of architecture for creating cairn heights.

Sens of direction

Each manhir has been so erected that the finished surfaces face north and the unfinished south. These menhirs have been further subjected to putting them in east or west inclination. They have also been shaped in

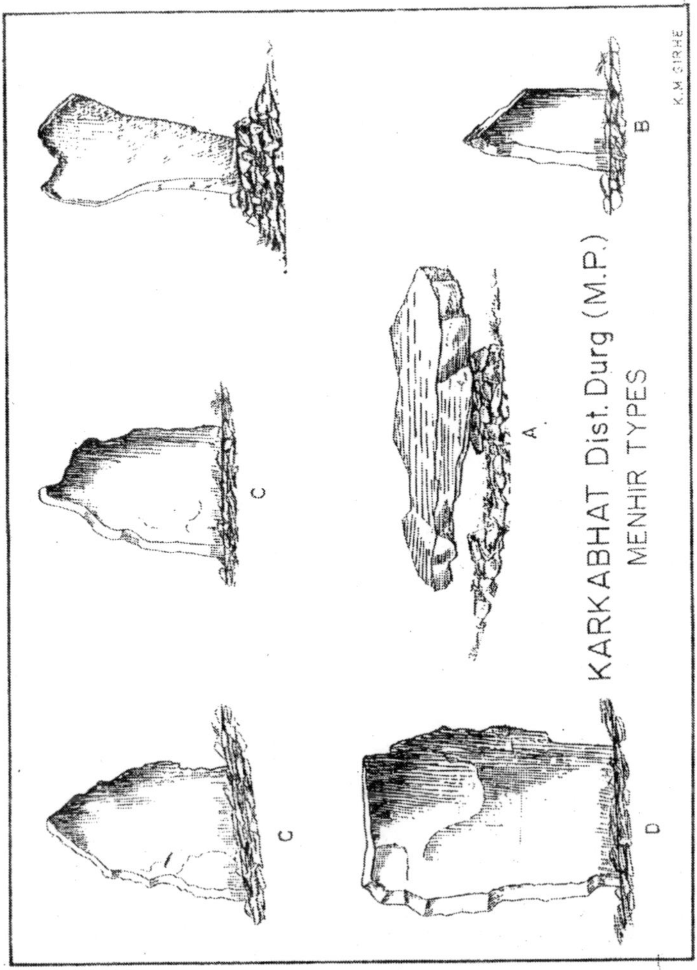

Fig. 20 : Menhir - Shapes

such a fashion that either they are conical pointing upwards or their top end is fashioned obliquely, the pointed end pointing either to the east or to the west. The angle of deviation from the magnetic north shows that htey were diliberately so erected that they indicate about the sense of direction and solar position. It is not necessary that these memorial menhirs were erected immediately after the death of the person. They might have been erected even after a lapse of time but that position indicates the time and period of the year when the deceased left the world.

Shape of menhirs

A. Fish shaped : (Pl. XIII, Fig. 20-A)

In this type one end is pointed whereas the other is bifurcated in the form of a tail of a fish. In case of standing menhirs of this type bifurcated end is towards the top whereas in case of capstones it is towards north.

B. Obliquely Pointed : (Pl. XXXII A, Fig. 20-B)

Top of menhir is obliquely pointed with the pointed end towards east or west.

C. Conical : (Pl. XXXII B, Fig. 20-C)

The top of menhir is conical and erected in such a way that the magnetic line passes through the pointed end of the menhir.

D. Straight : (Pl. XI, Fig. 20-D)

The top of menhir is horizontally straight and flat with magnetic line passing through the centre of the width.

During the course of excavation, the following notable features were observed :-

1. All the circles/oblongs and menhirs are oriented north-south, i.e. in case of circles/oblongs length is north-south, whereas all menhirs are having their finished smooth surface facing north.
2. In almost all cases northern fringe of the cairn circle, upto atleast 1/3 of the circle, is lined with bigger size of boulders. This indicates that the front of each burial was towards north and of the four directions north was given more importance.
3. Presence of multiple stone circles of smaller size in the main cairn circle, with one or two stump like stones in the centre. In one case, these smaller circles belonging to different phases have been noticed. From some of these smaller circles pottery of thin grey ware and rough Black and Red ware have been recovered.

4. Erection of multiple menhirs (more than two) within one cairn circle at different time intervals as indicated by difference in the levels of foundation pits and subsequent enlargements of the outer lining of the cairn by big boulders are indicative of family burials. Moreover, separate groups of offerings below different menhirs also indicate in this direction.
5. Evidences indicate that the offering were normally kept inside the small stone circles around one of the menhirs.

The Sculptured menhir
(Pl. XXXIII & XXXIV, Fig. 21)

The most startling and important find is the sculptured menhir. Almost at the highest point in the area of memorials one of thc biggest menhir was found to be sculptured giving the profile of a man. The sculpted menhir has been put in the centre of cairn heap. Above the cairn heap the available height of the menhir is 2.57 m and width is 1.91 m. It has been erected in perfect north south position, i.e. widthwise east-west with the finished surface looking to the north and sculpted edge towards east. The masterly stroke of the sculptor has brought out a magnificent facial view of a man having receeding broad forehead, with prominent glabella point, sharp long nose, broad and prominent ridge in the upper

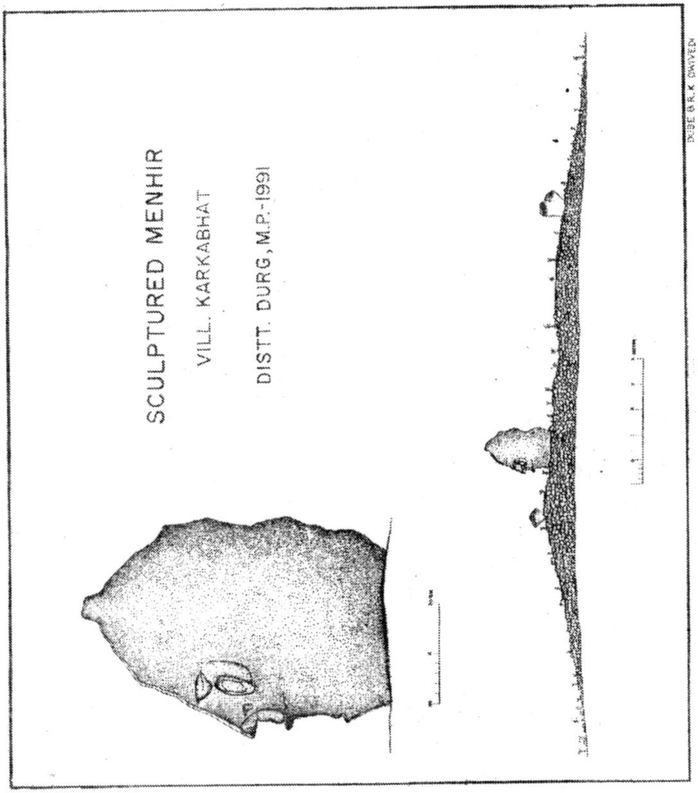

Fig. 21 : The Sculptured Menhir

lip below nasal spine, pronounced lower lip and protruded chin. On the northern face eye has also been carved out. A look at the southern surface of the menhir also shows the evidences of workmanship to create the profile. In the absence of chisel marks, it is at the moment difficult to find out the type of tool or tools used by the master sculptor to prepare the grand profile.

Though anthropomorphic forms of menhirs have been reported from some sites, e.g. Ramapuram, Karkabhat has the distinction of having, so far, the only sculpted menhir in the form of a human figure showing details of facial profile. Some scholars may argue that the menhir might have been shaped into sculpture, later and not by the megalithic people who erected it. Absence of any waste flakes around the menhir indicated that it was worked upon and carved out to create human facial profile before its installation in the cairn heap.

7

THE NUCLEUS AREAS

A. Karkabhat

Location of hundreds of Menhirs, capstones, cairn circles in the region of Karkabhat-Dhanora, spread over an area of nearly 5 sq.km. and complete absence of any other such concentration west of Mahanadi, in an area of at least 50 sq.km., it appears, that Karkabhat-Dhanora, due to its ideal location, easy accessibility, plenty of water and raw material for shaping and erecting megaliths, served as a nucleus point for performing the last rites of the departed souls whose mortal ramains were disposed of either by cremation or by some other means. In the absence of any skeletal remains and burials in the area for which Karkabhat served as a nucleus point, creamation seems to be the most probable way. It was not necessary to erect these memorials immediately after the death of the person, these could be erected even later, when there used to be collective gathering at Karkabhat, depending on various religious, social and economic factors. There must have been a central religious authority to decide and declare the dates and control the whole affair. A similar parallel is found amongst one of the tribes in Bastar today who erect memorial stones at one particular spot. This function was organised in May-June 1991 after a gap of nearly twenty-five years, when people even from Maharashtra also participated and after elaborate religious rites, erected memorial stones in honour of the departed ones, who left this world even twenty-five years back.

B. Other areas

During the course of recent explorations, another Megalithic nucleus area of Karkabhat dimensions was located east of Mahanadi on its right bank in Aroud-Lilar-Bhawarmara area. (Pl. XXXV A). here also, like Karkabhat area, hundreds of megaliths and cairn circles of all varieties are available. A survey of nearly 50 sq. km. of area east of Mahanadi in this region, did not reveal any other megalithic remains. It appears that Aroud-Lilar-Bhawarmara area served as a nucleus area for megalithic people, east of Mahanadi. Further eastwards along the river Mahanadi, 16 kms. north of Basna town in district Mahasamund, another cluster of menhirs was recently located in village Bartia-bhata. (Pl. XXXVI). There are 600 to 700 of them in a cluster. But as compared to above mentioned two areas, at Bartia-bhata only menhirs have been erected. There are no cairn heaps and stone circles around the menhirs. Secondly, the menhirs are comparatively smaller in size (1.00 to 1.5 m above G.L.) than those found at Karkabhat and Aroud. The Bartia-bhata menhirs which are also in distinct groups, resemble more to those found in Bastar district (Pl. XXXV B) and Hazaribagh district of Bihar. (Pl. XXXVII A). Some of these menhirs were dug up during laying of road and construction of students hostel and from below the menhirs iron objects like daggers, spearheads, knives, arrow-heads, etc. were recovered.

Dating

So far no dates are available for megalithic period in Chhattisgarh region. On the basis of iron tool typology and pottery, particularly Black-and-Red ware from Sorar, which are dated elsewhee, megalithic memorials at Karkabhat could be dated to around 1st half of first millenium B.C. Absolute dates are awaited.

8

EPILOGUE

Though a large number of megalithic sites have been explored and reported from the fertile land of Chhattisgarh region, in the absence of any large scale scientific excavations, the caltural identity of these sites and their relationship with those of other areas, including the far flung areas of North East India, Chotta Nagpur plateau of Bihar, etc. were not clear. A short excavation was conducted by Dr. M.G. Dikshit at Dhanora, District Durg, M.P. in 1956-57, but due to extremely limited nature of the excavation not much inferences could be drawn. Bastar is one of the regions where the megalithic traditions of the past still continues. The ethrographical studies of these prevailing traditions along with the data collected from the excavations at Karkabhat, have to a greater extent helped in understanding the nature and cultural traditions of the megalithic people of Chhattisgarh vis-a-vis with other regions.

So far as the ceramic evidences from Sorar and data in respect of metal objects are concerned, they show a close resemblance with the sites excavated in Vidarbha region of Maharashtra. The megalithic people around Karkabhat and other areas in Chhattisgarh honoured their departed souls by creating cairn heaps, erecting elaborate memoraials in the form of Menhirs of different shapes and sizes and by offering some weapons and ornaments loved by them. It is remarkable that even after years of death, they remembred them and performed elaborate, expensive rites. The nature and dimension of memorials erected speak of the collective effort of the communities involved. This would have been possible only with the existence of a homogenous society with perfect understanding of norms laid down and executed under the leadership of all respected religious authority. There was no question of deviating from the norms which speaks of a perfect disciplined society.

The people of Karkabhat area seemed to have lived both in natural habitats like low rock shelters and in huts with clay walls and lime and clay floorings in which wooden posts supported the roof of straw and grass above. The floors of the houses were repaired periodically. They used various types of ceramics, chief of which were Black-and-Red ware, rough ware of thick fabrics. Main forms were bowls, dishes and storage pots. They practised a mixed economy, partly agriculturists and partly hunters and gathers as could be seen from the variety of iron weapons of offensive and an iron ploughshare found from excavations. As in the dense forest allround there was plenty of game, hunting of not so dangerous animals was not difficult. In the absence of animal bones from the megalithic burials, it is difficult to say whether the megalithic people of this region also practised animal husbandry. For this we have to expose larger deposits of this period in Sorar.

They were skilled artisans. They knew smelting of iron from the rich ore available nearly in plenty. Variety of iron objects like dagger blades, spear-heads, spikes, arrow-heads, ploughshare speak of their skill. The well fabricated tools show that they had acquired mastery over iron technology of the times. Recovery of few gold and silver ornaments indicate that they were in contact with other people in the adjoining areas who had the better knowledge of these metals and their formulations.

As is clear from the layout of the cairn circles, cairn-heaps created by receeding number of small stone circles, boulder and clay fillings, from bottom upwards, cutting, shaping and erection of menhirs that they had well defined elaborate system of funerary rituals. Though the memorials were also erected after a considerable gap of time between the death of the persons and performance of ritual rites, they meticulously observed the timings of death while shaping and erecting these memorials. This is evident from the fact that the menhirs are pointed and inclined at a particular angle. They observed and kept in mind the seasonal position of the sun. It will not be too far to imagine that they had a well knit family system as could be seen from multiple menhirs erected in a single cairn heap. Life long adherance and loyalty to a single wife appears to be a respected practice as could be seen from the 'D' type of burials where two menhirs are erected side by side in the cairn circle.

There used to be one chief, commanding the heighest social and religious status. Extraordinary of them were respected by erecting sculptured menhir in their honour. This is evident from the discovery of a sculpted menhir almost at the highest point and in the centre of the memorial area at Karkabhat.

That the people observating this megalithic culture occupied a larger area in Chhattisgarh-Bastar region is clear from various nucleus centres discovered n the area. The culture spread north and eastwards and prospered is evident from the occurance of sites in Hazaribagh district of Bihar, Assam, Nagaland, Meghalaya (Pl. XXXVII B), Manipur etc. The culture in course of time became so deep rooted that in above mentioned areas they are still being practiced by the aborigins (Pl. XXXVII B), probably as elaborately as was practised nearly 3000 years back. In all these areas there was a homogenous cultural substratum for more than one thousand years. Though so far no C-14 dates are available from different levels of dig at Karkabhat and Sorar, but the extraordinary large number of megaliths in each nucleus area also substantiate that the culture flourshed for a very long time. On the basis of similarities of antiquities from other dated sites, it could reasonably be deducted that this culture flourished in the area during 1st millenium B.C., simultaneously with megalithic culture of adjoining east Vidarbha region and possibly with the regions in Deccan, central and north-east India.

As no skeletal remains were recovered from any of the burials, it is clear that most probably cremation or the practice of leaving the body in open to be taken care of by nature, was/were the mode/s of disposal of the dead. In the absence of any skeletal remains, it is also not possible to know about the ethnic traits of the people who practised these rituals in various nucleus areas in Chhattisgarh. But on the basis of the data available for the tribal people in Bastar and Chhattisgarh region who still practice the elaborate custom of erection of memorials, we may surmise that these ethnic groups probably constituted the group in the past also. But for definite conclusions, large areas need to be excavated, yielding greater number of antiquities and skeletal remains. In order to understand the habitational traits of megalithic people of this region, it will be rewarding to expose a large area of this period at Sorar.

9

RETROSPECT

In the end it will be worthwhile to give in brief the opinions of various scholars about the origin and distribution of Megaliths in India so that the reader could formulate his own opinion as the problem to some extent sill persists. Of course, through recent researches and unbiased views, by and large, the earlier opinion of megalithic culture reaching India from east or west or from both, is being slowly discarded. It is now being widely accepted that the culture originated and developed in the sub-continent, independently, probably evolving from Neolithic cultures of the area concerned. There were internal migrations and in the process the local traits and traditions were acquired and assimilated. In the case introduction of iron technology also, there is now no doubt, in the light of results of excavations at Gufkral, in Jammu and Kashmir, that the megalithic people in this part of the country possessed the knowledge of iron around 1500 B.C. Similar developments of iron technology, in other areas also took place, probably a little later, in other areas.

With the excavation of cist burials yielding iron in Almora and wide spread occurance of Black-and-Red ware, throughout the country, associated with megalithic culture, there is now no doubt that from 1500 B.C. to around the beginning of the Christian era, megalithic monuments were a witness to highly advanced state of civilization with cultural affinity throughout the length and breadth of the country with knowlede of iron and community living well entrenched.

Huttan, J.H. through his various articles expresses the view that the elaborately carved forked and cylindrical monoliths of Dimapur in Nagaland are closely linked with the parallel ceremony of the Angami Nagas and similar to Munda monoliths in Chota Nagour. He is also of the view that the conch ornaments worn by Nagas and also found from the Odugattur graves have affinities with Sough Indian ones. In "Prehistory of Assam" (1928), he states that the Dolmens in Assam came from South India across the Bay of Bengal.

Professor Elliot Smith holds the view that the megaliths had their beginning in the proto-Dynastic Egypt from where it spread to other places. Walhouse and others advocate a western origin. Longhurst favours an Egyptian-like culture which produced megaliths in the Deccan around 1000 B.C.

Hunt, E.H. in his papers on "Hyderabad Cairn burials and their significance" (1929), and "Megalithic burials in South India" (1933), found external association and possible foreign influence on the basis of presence of beads of lapis-lazuli in the burials.

Ghurye, G.S. in his article on 'Funerary monuments of India' (1926), states that Indian Megaliths are intimately connected with the Egyptian funerary mouments. On the basis of architectural development these burials are dated to 1000 B.C. He is also of the view that India is the home proper of the dolmens.

Haimendrof, C. Von E while desribing Megalithic ritual among the Gadabas and Bondos of Orissa (1943) states that the megalithic monuments and rites of the Gadabas and Bondos fit well into the general picture of the megalithic civilization of South East Asia. The similarity of these with the Assam megaliths both in the underlying idea and nature of monuments stress that the megalithic culture of Orissa is a branch of that megalithic civilization which is so widely distributed in South East Asia. He is of the view that the migrations took place in neolithic times and they did not penetrate beyond the Godavari.

In his paper on 'The problem of megalithic cultures of Middle India' (1945), Haimendrof further states that the purpose and meaning of the megalithic monuments of the Gadabas and Bondos have the same basic idea as that of the Assam tribes. The connecting links between the Gonds and the Nagas is to be found in the forked 'Y' posts. (A huge 'Y' forked mehir is also present at Karkabhat - author.) Similarities of customs and rituals are found between the middle Indian and north-east Indian tribes. He is of the opinion that the megalithic culture of the South East Asiatic type found among the Gadabas, Bondos and the Bastar Gonds come from the east with its centre of diffusion in eastern Assam or north Burma or south-west China. The people speaking Austronesian languages are connected with this culture. It is quite likely that there was an earlier migration of Austroasiatic culture untouched by the Austronesian. This megalithic culture was already developed before the commencement of the migration of Austroasiatic races westwards into peninsular India. The author discounts the Dravidian speakers as possible representatives of the megalithic culture of South East Asiatic affinity. But after nearly ten years the same author in his article, "New aspects of the Dravidian Probelm" (1953), revises his opinion and says that the Iron Age megalithic builders were Dravidian speakers. This iron using culture in South India was an intrusion superimposing itself on the more primitive indegenous cultures and iron did not come from the north. He postulated a theory of immigration by sea or southward movement along the west coast of India some time about 700-400 B.C.

Aiyappan, A. in his Presidential Address in XXXIInd (1945) session of Indian Science Congress Association pointed out that (i) Megaliths have a world wide distribution, (ii) different types of monuments, even though belonging to the same period reflected cultural diversity and (iii) since megaliths are still being practised by certain Indian tribes, they could not have been a sudden exotic introduction.

Srinivasan, K.R. in his article on "Indian Megaliths with special reference to Pudukkottai" (1944), expresses the view that neither the Vedic-Aryans nor the Indus people were responsible for these monuments. He states that Tamil literature is replete with ample evidence for the knowledge of this cult from atleast 1000 B.C. Survival of this cult and the knowledge of iron among some primitive tribes in the south and central India would suggest an earlier period, probably 2500-1000 B.C. He also indicates Egyptian origin for this cult. He also states that the megalithic monuments bear witness to a highly advanced state of civilization with knowledge of iron and community living.

Yazdani, G. (1917), while examining some peculiar marks on the pottery from megalithic burials of the Deccan, remarked that these megaliths of South India resembled those of Etrucia. He stated that possibly the early settlers brought with them the mode of megalithic tomb-building, speech and semi-hieroglyphs, which perhaps, was gradually modified by local and foreign influence. The megalith-builders migrated via Makran, where similar sepulchres and a dialect-Bruhi akin to Dravidian is to be seen.

Subbarao, B in "Megalithic Problem of South India and the Dravidian Language", (1962) is of the opinion that the megalithic cult was adopted or introduced into South India by a people who had already come into contact with the Iron Age people in northern and central India. Maritime movement theory is not acceptable to the author. He indicates terrestrial movement from north to south. Regarding the theory of eastern origin for the megaliths, he feels that central and south India was meeting place of ideas and cultures from the east as well as west. He is of the opinion that linguistic evidence indicates to mutual assimilation of words between Dravidian and Sanskritic languages. He does not favour the idea of evolution of megalithic iron Age people out of the earlier neolithic stock. He postulates that the Dravidians seemed to have moved southwards and eastwards from Rajasthan across central to South India.

N.R. Banerjee, while discussing the Megalithic problem of Chigleput concludes that there was a settled community life, perhpas the result of mutual contact, trade, etc. with others or perhaps due to the ethnic and cultural homogeneity of megalithic-practicing people. They knew smelting and forging of iron for their implements and weapons. They believed in life after death.

While discussing the 'Chronology of Megaliths in south India', Banerjee further states that the impact of the neolithic and the chalcolithic periods (1500-80 B.C.) would effect the chronology of the megaliths in South India. He is of the opinion that the Dravidian speakers were indigenous people inhabiting the whole of the Indo-Pakistan sub-continent.

While describing the human remains from Megaliths of Yelleswaram, Pabitra Gupta and Pratap Dutta state that 'the general morphology and the metric characters did not favcur an autochthonous theory but indicate to Scytho-Iranian affinity. This supports the view expressed by S.S. Sarkar after examing human skeletal remains from Brahmagiri. He concluded that the crania from megaliths reveal an autochtonous Australoid type and a more or less medium statured mesocephotic, medium vaulted flat nose type with robust constitution and powerful upper and lower jaws probably of the Scytho-Iranian stocks.

Dikshit, K.N. in his Seminar Paper on "The Origin and distribution of Megaliths in India", (1969) opines tha the Indian megaliths appear to contain different traits introduced by different peoples at different times. While some of the types seem to have been imported, quite a few evolved independently. Urn-burial and inhumation in pits are indigenous contributions of the neolithic-chalcolithic communities of South India. It is likely that the Western Asiatic Maritime communities practicing megalithic architecture entered South India through the Persian Gulf or Southern Arabia.

Ramchandran, K.S. (1969) feels that inspite of a chronological gap of 1700 years, the Megalithic Rock-cut caves in Kerala were as a result of contact with west Asia, around 1000 B.C. The variance in burial furnishings were probably due to their mingling with the local population and assimilation of their traits and funerary traditions. He points out that iron diffused into India from the north and the west coast.

Purshottam, Singla (1969), is of the view that the megaliths of North-Western India and South India have no relationship whatsoever.

Soundara Rajan, K.V., (1969) is of the view that Megalithism might have arrived into India from more than one source but only from the west and equally by overland route, along the coasts or across the sea. The megalithic types of Uttar Pradesh are not genetically related to tomb-architecture with the peninsular megalithic types.

While commenting on the paper 'Prehistoric Remains in Central India' by Rivelt, Carnac, J.H., in 1979 Mr. Blandord observed that the peculiar and restricted distribution of burial circles seen at Junapani, near

Nagpur, would indicate their attribution to an immigrant race and not from aboriginal tribe. The shaffle bits and stirrups would connect the circle-building race with the tribes of Central Asia, who have been horsemen from time immemorial. None of the wilder tribes of Indian peninsula used horses and it is not indigenous to the country.

SELECT BIBLIOGRAPHY

Agrawal, D.P., Kusumgar, S. and Sara, R.P., 'Radio Carbon dates of Archaeological samples', *Current Science,* Vol. 33, No. 9, 1964.

Aiyappan, A., "The Megalithic Culture of South India", in *Indian Science Congress Association XXXII* (1945), *Presidential Address :* Anthropology and Archaeology Section.

Aiyappan, A., "Rude Stone Monuments of the Perumal Hills - Kodaikanal, *Quarterly Journal of the Mythic Society,* Bangalore, 1940-41.

Allchin, F.R., "The Stone Alignment of Southern Hyderbad" in *Man.* LVI (1956).

Allchin, F.R. Piklihal Excavations, *Andhra Pradesh Government Archaeological Series,* No. 1 (Hyderabad, 1960).

Allchin, B&R, *The Birth of Indian Civilization,* Penguin Books Ltd., Harmondsworth, Middlesex, England, 1968.

Ancient India, No. 13, 1957.

Ancient India No. 20-21, 1967.

Babington, J., "Description of the Pandoo Coolies in Malabar", in *Transactions of the Literary Society of Bombay III* (1823).

Bali, V., 'Stone monuments in the District Singhbhum, Chota Nagpur' in *Indian Antiquary* I (1872).

Banerjee, N.R. "Amrithmangalam, District Chingleput" in *Indian Antiquary,* 1954-55.

Banerjee, N.R. and K.V. Soundara Rajan, "Sanur 1950 & 52 : A Megalithic site in District.Chingleput" in *Ancient India,* No. 15 (New Delhi, 1959).

Banerjee N.R., *Iron Age in India*, 1967.

Banerjee N.R., 'The Chronology of the megaliths of South India', Proceedings of the *First International Conference on Asian Archaeology.*

Bidie, "Prehistoric graves near Pallavaram" in *Journal of Royal Asiatic Society,* XXX (1967).

Blakiston, J.F. (ed.), "Departmentl routine notes" in *Annual Report of the Archeological Survey of India",* 1924-25.

Boswell, J.A., "On the ancient remains in the Krishna District : Scythic remains of sepulchure" in *Indian Antiquary* I (1872).

Branfill, B.R., "Rude Megalithic monuments in North Arcot" in *Journal of Asiatic Society of Bengal* (1880).

Branfill, B.R., "On thc Savandurga Rude Stone Cemetery, Central Maisur" in *Indian Antiquary,* X (1881).

Breeks, J.W., *An account of the Primitive tribes and monuments of the Nilgiris* (London, 1837).

Burgess, Jas, "The Dolman at Konur and Aihole" in *Indian Antiquary* III (1874).

C. Von Furer - Haimendrof, 'The Problem of Megalithic Culture in Middle India', *Man in India,* Vol. 25 (1945).

Carlyle, A.C.L., "A tour in Eastern Rajputana in 1871-72 and 1972-73", *Report of the Archaeological Survey of India,* VI (1878).

Childe, Gordar V., "Megaliths" in *Ancient India* No. 4 (New Delhi, 1948), pp. 5-13.

Childe, V. Gordan, *New Light on the Most Ancient East,* (London, 1954).

Codrington, K. de B., 'Indian Cairn and Urn burials' in *Man,* XXX (1930).

Coggin Brown, J.C., "Note on Cinerary urns found in the Mundai country" in *Journal of Bihar and Orissa Research Society,* I (1915).

Coghlam, H.H., *Notes on Prehistoric and Early Iron in the Old World* (Oxford, 1956).

Cousens, H., "Lists of Antiquarian Remains in the Central Provinces and Benar" in *Report of the Archaeological Survey of India,* XIX (1897).

Cunningham, A., "A Tour in the Central Provinces in 1873-74 and 1874-75", in *Report of the Archaeological Survey of India,* IX (1879).

Dalton, E.T., "Rude Stone Monuments in Chotta Nagpur and Other Places" in *Journal of the Asiatic Society of Bengal,* XLII (1873).

Deo, S.B., "Excavations at Khapa and Takalghat, District Nagpur" in *Indian Archaeology* 1967-68 - *A Review.*

Deo, S.B., "Megaliths in Maharasthra", *Seminar Papers on the Problem of Megaliths in India,* (Varanasi, 1969).

Deo, S.B., *Paunar Excavations,* Nagpur, 1968.

Desikan, Srinivasa V.N., "Exploration in District Coimbatore" in *Indian Archaeology* 1961-62 - *A Review.*

Dhavalikar, M.K., "A Plough coulter from Brahmagiri (India)", *Antiquary* XLIL (1968).

Dikshit, M.G., "Excavation at Dhanora, District Durg" in *Indian Archaeology* 1956-57 — *A Review.*

Dikshit, M.G., *Excavations at Kaundinyapura.*

Dikshit, K.N., "Megalithic Typology and Chronology — A Restatement" in *Samskriti* (1968).

Dikshit, K.N., "The Origin and Distribution of Megaliths in India" in *Seminar Papers* (1969).

Department of Ancient History and Archaeology, University of Madras, "Exploration in District Trichchirappalli", in *Indian Archaeology* — 1961-62 — *A Review.*

Department of Archaeology, University of Madras, "Exploration in District Thanjavr" in *Indian Archaeology* — 1964-65 — *A Review.*

Director of Archaeology, Hyderabad, "Burial sites etc., Hyderabad Near Topran a village in District Medak" in *Indian Archaeology* — 1953-54 — *A Review.*

Director, Department of Archaeology, Kerala State, "Megaliths, District Kozhikode", "Megaliths Districts Quilon and Palghat and "Rock-cut-Caves, District Trichur" in *Indian Archaeology* — 1961-62 — *A Review.*

Elwin, V., "Funerary Customs in Bastar State" in *Man in India* XXV (1945).

Fergusson, James, *"Rude Stone Monuments in All Countries" Their Age and Usage"*, 1872.

Garrick, "Report of a tour in the Punjab and Rajputana" in 1883-84 in *Report of the Archaeological Survey of India*, XXIII (1887).

Gaur R.C., "Megalithic Tradition in India", in *Seminar Papers* (1969).

Ghurya, G.S., "Funerary Monuments of India" in *Man in India,* VI (1926).

Gopal Lallanji, 'Antiquity of Iron in India', *Uttar Bharati,* Vol. IX, No. 3.

Grigson, V.W., *The Maria Gonds of Bastar,* (London, 1938).

Gupta, S.P., "Sociology of Burial Practices and its bearing on the problem of megaliths", in *Seminar Papers* (1969).

Gururaja Rao, B.K., *Megalithic Culture in South India,* Mysore, 1972.

Haimendrof, C. Von E., "Megalithic ritual among the Gadabas and Bondos of Orissa" in *Journal of Asiatic Society of Bengal,* IX (1943).

Haimendorf, C. Von F., "The Problem of Megalithic Cultures of Middle India" in *Man in India,* XXV (1945).

Haimendrof, C. Von F., "New Aspects of the Dravidian Problem" in *Tamil Culture,* II (1953).

Hunt, E.H., "Hyderabad Cairn Burials and their Significance" in *Journal of the Royal Anthropological Institute of Great Britain and Ireland,* 54 (1929).

Hunt, E.H., Megalithic Burials in South India, *Journal of the Royal Asiatic Society,* 1953.

Hutton, J.H., "Carved Monoliths at Dimapur and An Angami Naga Ceremony" and "The Meaning and Method of the Erection of Monoliths by the Naga Tribes", *Journal of the Royal Anthropological Institute of Great Britain and Ireland,* 52 (1922).

Hutton, J.H., "Some Megalithic Work in Jantia Hills", in *Journal of Asiatic Society of Bengal",* XXII (1926).

Hutton, J.H., "Naga Chank Ornaments and South Indian Affinities" in *Man,* XXVI (1926).

Hutton, J.H., "Prehistory of Assam" in *Man in India,* VIII (1928).

Hutton J.H., "The Meaning and Method of the Erection of Monoliths by the Naga Tribes", *Journal of the Royal Anthropological Institute,* Vol. III (1922).

Iyer, Krishna, L.A., "The Significance of Megalithic Monuments" in *Quarterly Journal of the Mythic Society,* Bangalore, XXIX (1938-39).

India, A Regional Geography Ed. R. R.L. Singh. Varanasi, 1971.

Indian Archaeology — 1956-57 — *A Review.*

Khan, Abdul Waheed, "A Monograph on Yeleswaram Excavations", *Andhra Pradesh Archaeological Series,* XIV (Hyderabad, 1963).

Kosambi, D.D., "The beginning of the Iron Age in India", *Journal of the Economic and Social History of the Orient,* Vol. VI, Pt. III, (Leidon, 1963).

Krishnaswami V.D. and B. Saran, "Excavations at Kunnattur, District Chingleput", in *Indian Archaeology* — 1957-58 — *A Review.*

Krishnaswamy, V.D., "Typology of Indian Megaliths", in *Ancient India,* No. 5, 1949.

Lewis, A.L., "Notes on the builders and the purpose of megalithic monuments, in *Report of the British Association for Advancement of Science — Transactions,* 1869.

Mitra, P., "The Indian Megaliths — Their Origin and Chronology" in *Proceedings of the Asiatic Society of Bengal,* 1921.

Mukherjee, S.K., "Megaliths, Nagpur", in *Indian Archaeology* 1961-62 — *A Review.*

Narain, A.K. and P.C. Pant, "Excavation of Banimilia-Bahera, District Mirzapur" in *Indian Archaeology* — 1962-63 — *A Review.*

Narasimaiah, B., "Exploration in District North Arcot and Salem" in *Indian Archaeology* - 1964-65 — *A Review.*

Rao, S.R., "Excavation at Paiyampalli, Distt. North Arcot" in *Indian Archaeology* - 1964-65, 1067-68 — *A Review*.

Roy, David, "Megalithic Culture of the Khasis" in *Proceedings of the Indian Science Congress Association,* 1937.

Rybot, N.Y.L., "Groups of Menhir in Kashmir", in *Man.* XXXI (1931).

Ramachandran, K.S., "Chronology of the Indian Megaliths — Some Consideration" in *Puratattva,* No. 3 (1969-70).

Ramchandran, K.S., *A Bibliography on Indian Megaliths,* 1971.

Sankalia, H.D., "Excavation at Tekkalakoto, District Bellary" in *Indian Archaeology* - 196-64 — *A Review*.

Sardarilal and R.K. Pant, "Exploration in District Anantnag" in *Indian Archaeology* - 1962-63 — *A Review*.

Sarkar, H., "Excavation at Kesarapalli near Gannavaram, District Krishna", in *Indian Archaeology* - 1961-62 — *A Review*.

Sen Gupta, K.K., "On the Chronological Sequence of Some Megalithic Monuments" in *Journal of the Asiatic Society of Bengal,* XII (1916).

Sharma, B.K., "Megalithic Burials, Lohardanga, Distt. Ranchi", in *Indian Archaeology* - 1963-64 — *A Review*.

Sharma, G.R., "Excavations at Kotia, Distt. Allahabad", in *Indian Archaeology* - 1963-64 — *A Review*.

Sharma G.R., "Excavation at Hathinia Pahr, Kakoria and Bhadahawan Hillock, Distt. Varanasi, in *Indian Archaeology* - 1963-64 — *A Review*."

Shaw R.B., "Religious Cairns of the Himalayan Region", in

Report of the British Association for Advancement of Science — Transactaions, 1872.

Sinha, B.K., "Explorationi in District Chanda", in *Indian Archaeology — 1967-68 — A Review.*

Sircar, D.C., "The Dravidian Probelm" in *Man in India,* XXXV (1955).

Srinivasan, K.R., "The Megalithic Burial and Cairn fields of South India in the light of Tamil Literature and Tradition" in *Ancient India,* No. 2.

Srinivasan, K.R. and N. R. Banerjee, "Survey of South Indian Megaliths", in *Ancient India,* No. 9, (1953).

Sharma, Baijnath, "Megaliths in Hoshangabad, Narsinghpur and Jabalpur Districts of M.P." in *Seminar Papers,* 191969).

Singh, Purshottam, "Megaliths from North-Western India", in *Seminar Papers* (1968).

Singh, S.D., "Iron in Ancient India", *Journal of the Economic and Social History of the Orient,* Vol. V, Pt. II (Leiden, 1962).

Subbarao, B. *"The Personality of India"* (1958).

Subbarao, B., "Megalithic Problem of SouthIndia and the Dravidian Language" in *Transactions of Archaeological Society of South India, Silver Jubilee Volume* (1962).

Subbarao, B. "Archaeology and Anthropology in India" in *Indian Anthropology,* Essays in memory of D.N. Majumdar (Bombay, 1962).

Subbara, B., "Megalithic Problem of South India and the Dravidian Languages", *Trans. of the Archaeological Society of South India,* Silver Jubilee Volume (1962).

Sen, D.K., "Observations on the Megalithic Skeletal Remains", *Seminar Papers on the Problem of Megaliths in India* (Varanasi, 1969).

Subrahmanyam, R., "Excavation at Nagarjunakonda, District Guntur", in *Indian Archaeology* - 1959-60 — *A Review.*

Sundara, A., "Exploration in District Belgaum, Bijapur and Shimoga", in *Indian Archaeology* - 1967-68 — *A Review.* in *Seminar Papers (1969).*

Soundara Rajan, K.V., "Megaliths and the black and red ware" in *Seminar Papers* (1969).

Sundara, A., *"The Early Chamber Tombs of South India"*, Delhi, 1975.

Thapar, B.K., "Excavation at Junapatni", in *Indian Archaeology* - 1961-62 — *A Review.*

Thapar, B.K., "Parkalam 1948 — Excavation of a Megalithic Urn Burial" in *Ancient India,* No. 8 (1952).

Thapar, B.K., "Maski, 1954 : A Chalcolithic Site of the Souther Deccan", *Ancient India,* No. 13 (1957).

Thapar, B.K. "Prakash 1955 : A Chalcolithic Site in the Tapti Valley", *Ancient India,* Nos. 20 & 21 (1967).

Tripathy, K.C., "Megalithic Cultures of Orissa", in *Seminar Papers* (1969).

Walhouse, M.J., "Archaeological Notes — Curious Tombs and Entombments" in Indian Antiquary, VI (1877).

Walhouse, M.J., "Archaeological Notes in Sepulchral Customs, Existing and Prehistoric", in *Indian Antiquary,* VII *1878).

Walhouse, M.J., "Some non-Sepulchral Rude Stone Monuments in India, Peersia and Western Asia", in *Indian Antiquary* VIII (1879).

Watson John W., "A Rude Stone Monument in Gujarat" in *Indian Antiquary,* III (1874).

Wheeler, R.E.M., *"Early India and Pakistan"*, Ancient Peoples and Places XII (London, 1959).

Wheeler, Mortimer, Brahmagiri and Chanduvalli, 1947 : Megalithic and other Cultures in Mysore State, *Ancient India,* No. 4, 1947.

INDEX

Pl. I : General view of the site

Pl. II : General view of the site

Pl. III A : Rock shelter

Pl. III B : Rock shelter

Pl. IV : Sorar - section looking west

Pl. V : Sorar - Section looking south-east

Pl. VI A : General view of factory site

Pl. VI B : Close up of finished menhir

Pl. VII : Megalith Type 'A' - before excavation

Pl. VIII : Megalith Type 'B' - before excavation

Pl. IX : Megalith Type 'C' - before excavation

Pl. X : Megalith Type 'D' - before excavation

Pl. XI : Megalith Type 'E' - before excavation

Pl. XII : Megalith Type 'F' - before excavation

Pl. XIII : Megalith Type 'G' - before excavation

Pl. XIV : Megalith Type A-1 - showing opened quadrants

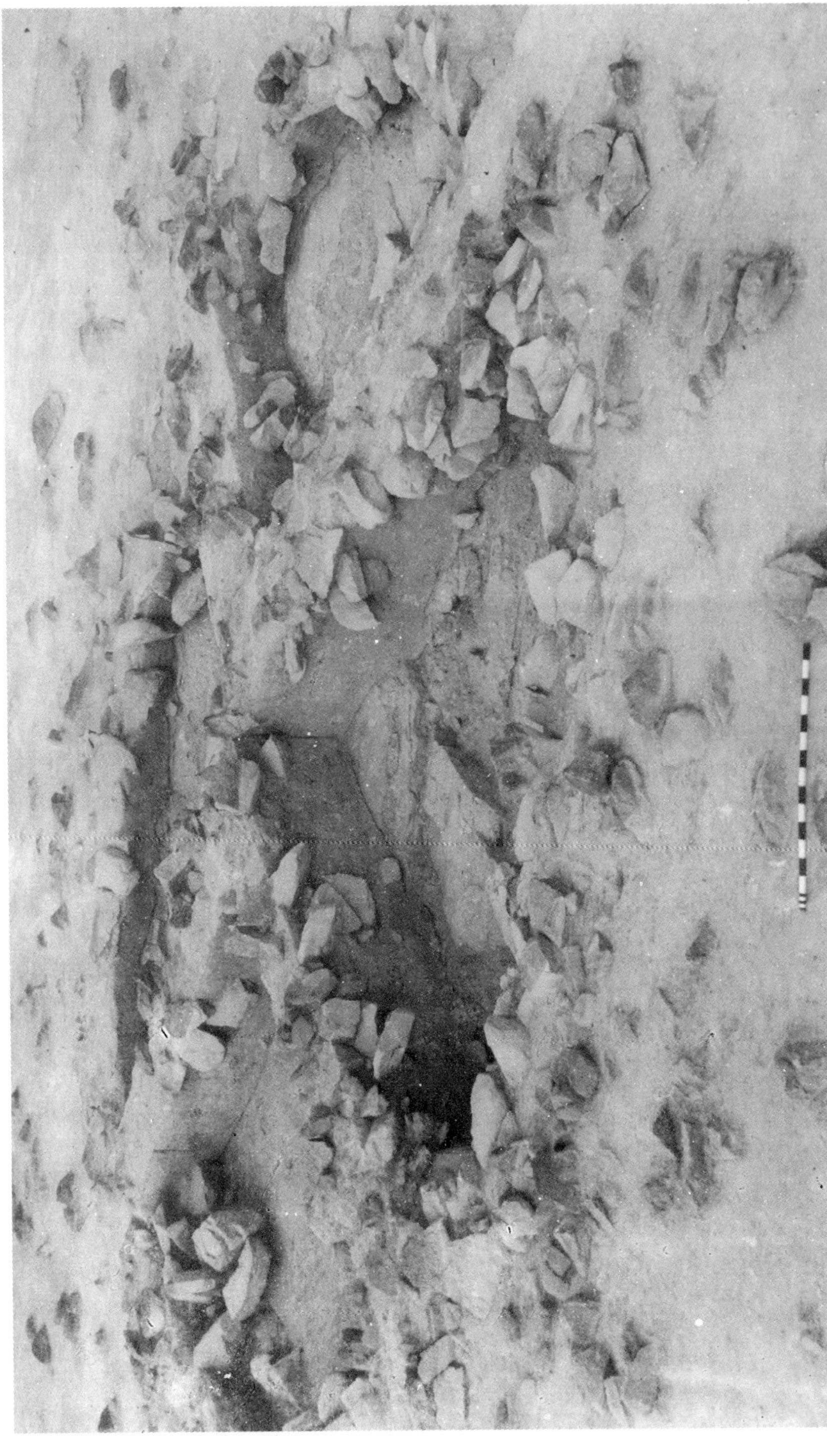

Pl. XV : Megalith Type A-2

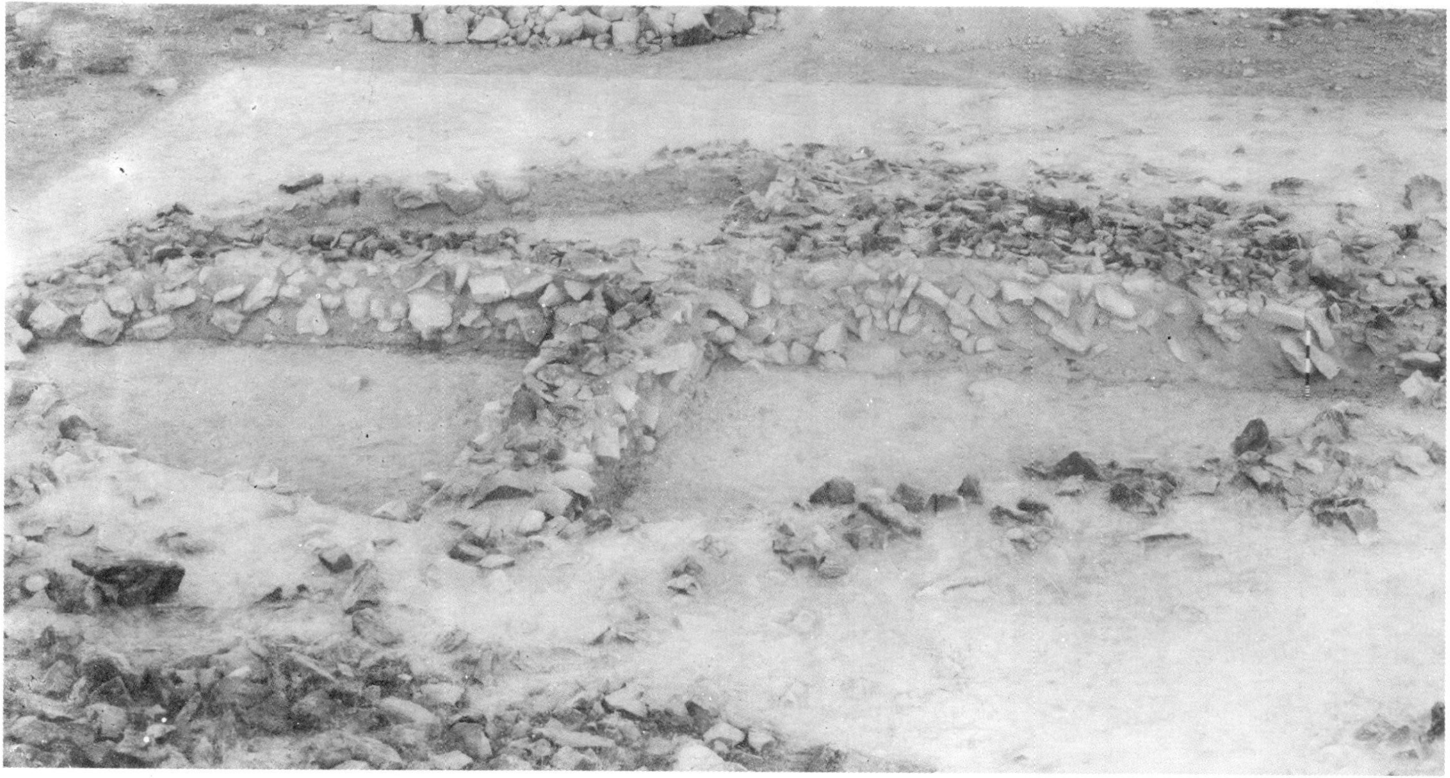

Pl. XVI : Megalith Type B-1

Pl. XVII : Megalith Type B-2

Pl. XVIII : Megalith Type C-1

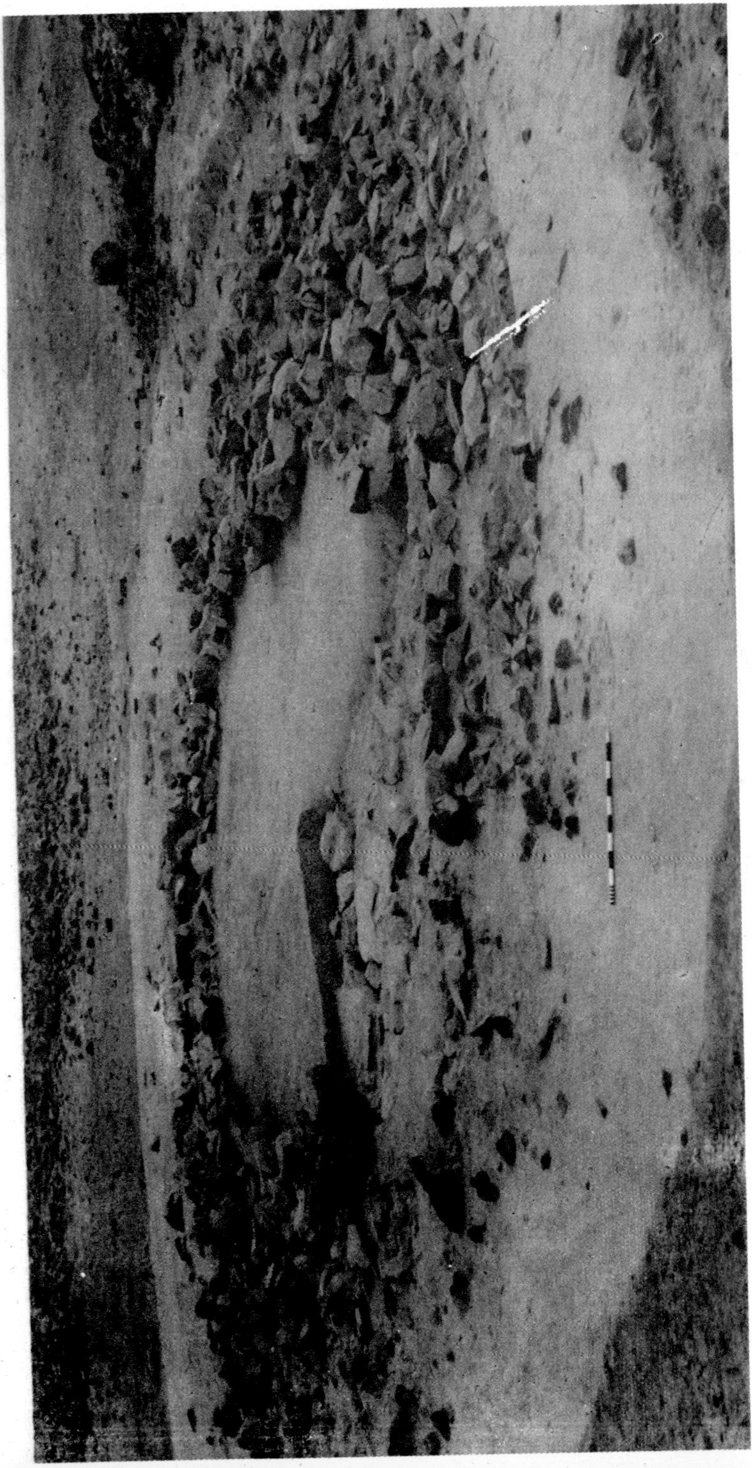

Pl. XIX : Megalith Type C-2

Pl. XX : Megalith Type D-1

Pl. XXII A : Megalith Type F-1-view from south

Pl. XVII B : Megalith Type E 1 view from east

Pl. XXIII : Megalith Type F-2

Pl. XXIV : Megalith Type G-1

Pl. XXV : Megalith Type G-2

Pl. XXVI A : Iron objects of offence

Pl. XXVI B : Spike and Dagger in-situ

Pl. XXVII A : Copper Bangles in-situ

Pl. XXVII B : Iron Plough share in-situ

Pl. XXVIII A : Arrow head in-situ

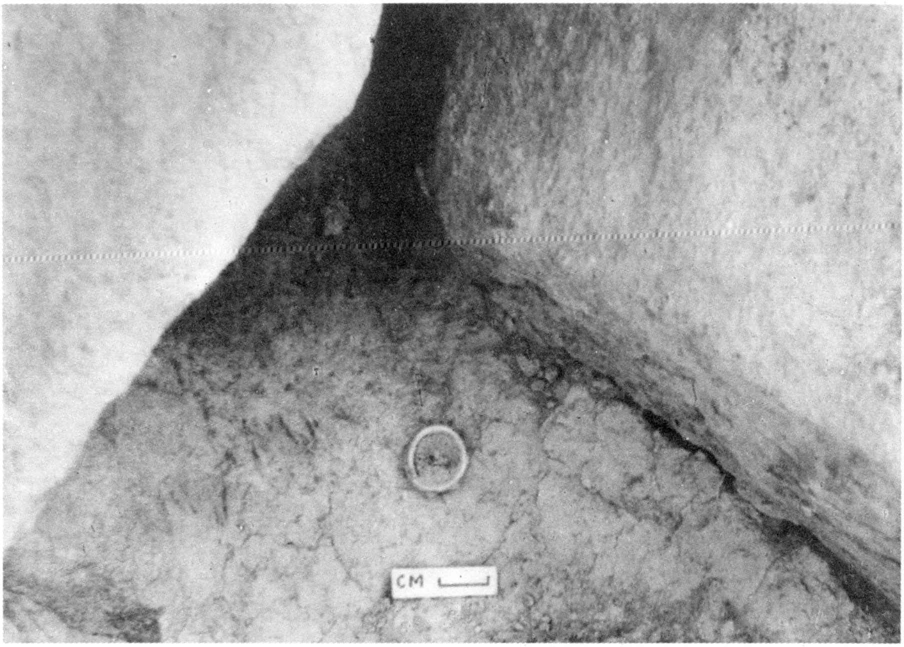

Pl. XXVIII B : Gold ring in-situ

Pl. XXIX A : Arrow heads

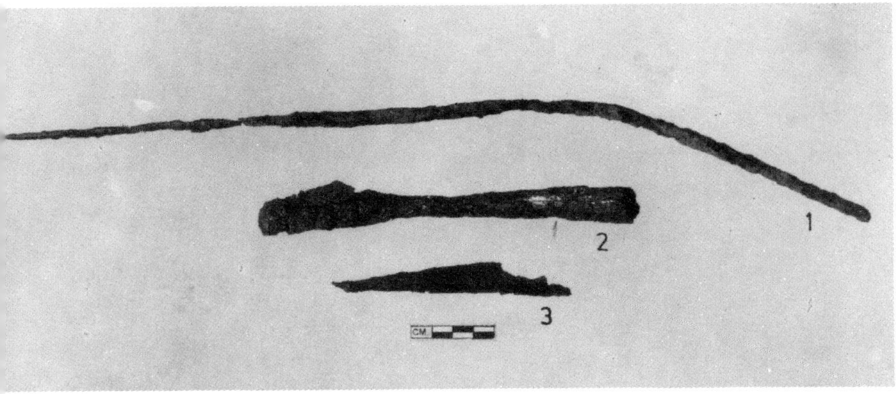

Pl. XXIX B : Spikes and spear head

Pl. XXX A : Plough share

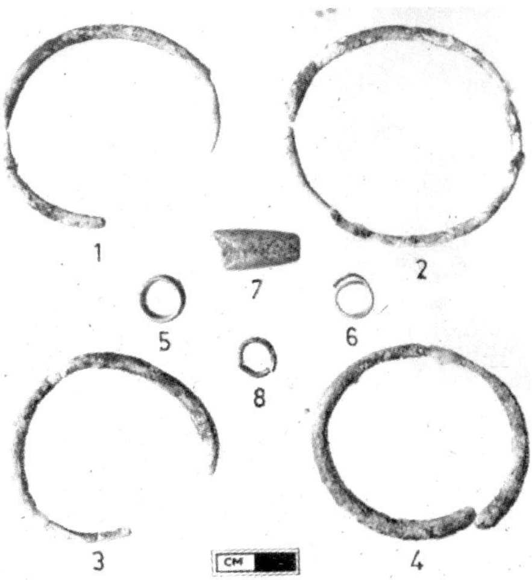

Pl. XXX B : Copper bangles 1-4, Gold ring 5&6
Silver ring 8, Stone bead 7

Pl. XXXI · Mini circles with central stone

Pl. XXXII A : Obliquely pointed menhir

Pl. XXXII B : Conical menhir

Pl. XXXIII : Sculptured menhir-northern face

Pl. XXXIV : Sculptured menhir-southern face

Pl. XXXV A : Megalith - Lilar - Aroud

Pl. XXXV B : Menhirs - Gammewada, Distt. - Bastar

Pl. XXXVI : Menhirs - Bartia Bhata, Distt. Mahasamud

Pl. XXXVII A : Menhirs, Distt. Hazaribagh, Bihar

Pl. XXXVII B : Menhirs, Bhoi country, Meghalaya

Pl. XXXVIII : Karkabhat, Modern burial